MW00650369

LIVE A

F.A.S.T.

LIFE

Fabulous.
Abundant.
Simple.
Tiny.

PRAISE FOR *LIVE A F.A.S.T. LIFE*

"I was fortunate enough to meet Jenn Baxter two years ago at a tiny house movement influencer event. Her professionalism, topical insight, social etiquette and inviting smile made her stand out in the room. I had no reason to believe her writing would be any different and I was excited to be asked to read an advance manuscript of this fantastic book. Jenn has lived an adult life that no one would envy. She has dealt with death, abuse, health threats and financial loss. She understands firsthand how debilitating life's problems can be. But through a set of life choices about everything from location and diet, to consumerism and faith, she has found a peace that truly passes understanding. Fortunately for us, she had decided to share her story and I, for one, felt so encouraged after reading it. I am sure you will as well."

Andrew M. Odom
Author, Speaker and Influencer

"If it is true that we are the sum total of our experiences, then Jenn Baxter is one tough chick. Women, in particular, often travel through life feeling lost and distracted by our pain. Jenn's story proves, once again, that it is not only possible to find strength and clarity from our pain, but the results can be positively inspirational. I highly recommend this book to anyone looking for a quick read that will motivate you to run F.A.S.T. in the direction of your dreams!"

Michelle "MJ" Boyle
Simple Life Advocate and Tiny House Podcast
Hostess with the Mostest

"Jenn Baxter is a heroine in the truest sense. Live a F.A.S.T. Life is her intimate story of perseverance — a heart-wrenching journey full of despair and, most importantly, hope. She reminds us that the imperfections, mistakes and heartache are a treasure trove of life lessons. In the end, Jenn's story is a call-to-action to focus on what matters most in life: your well-being and what brings you joy. This book left me feeling motivated — even fired up — to dig deeper into issues holding me back from living a healthier, more robust life. There's no time like now to embrace a higher quality of life and bucket-list living — an empowered yet grounded approach to living like every day is your last."

Alexis Stephens
Tiny House Expedition

"Jenn's mission is energizing, and her ability to gain strength from each trial is simply incredible. This is a story overflowing with a never-give-up, you-can-do-it message. It will inspire you to trade the cookie-cutter assumptions to explore the unique and creative plans God has for your life. Jenn's story will motivate you in living your story … and living it 'F.A.S.T.'!"

Heather Meadows
Writer and Speaker

"I couldn't wait to get my hands on this book, and it was worth all the anticipation! Written in a conversational style, it is full of tips and advice from a woman who has not simply survived, but also thrived. Jenn opens her closet and her heart to you! You will come away inspired to begin your own hero's journey."

Kari Cooper (also known as "Yurt Grrl")
Yurt and Tiny Living Expert

"The story of Jenn's downsizing journey is equal parts spiritual awakening and practical how-to guide. A great read if you're trying to cut the clutter and spark profound, lasting change in your own life."

Amy Henion
Writer and Simple Living Advocate

HOW STRIPPING DOWN & CLEANING UP GAVE ME MY LIFE BACK

LIVE A F.A.S.T. LIFE

Fabulous.
Abundant.
Simple.
Tiny.

JENN BAXTER

Live a F.A.S.T Life:
How Stripping Down & Cleaning Up Gave Me My Life Back

Copyright © 2017 by Jenn Baxter

All rights reserved.

Published by Silver Tree Publishing, a division of Silver Tree Communications, LLC (Kenosha, WI).
www.SilverTreeCommunications.com

All rights reserved. No portion of this book may be reproduced, scanned, sold, or distributed in any printed or electronic form without the express written permission of the author.

This book contains tips, advice and anecdotes about the author's own personal experiences with certain foods, consumer products, and medical and wellness treatments. The contents of this book do not constitute medical advice and should not replace your own judgment or the professional diagnosis, treatment or advice of your own healthcare practitioners.

Editing by:
Cathy Fyock
Andrew Odom
Michelle "MJ" Boyle
Kate Colbert

Cover design and typesetting by:
Courtney Hudson

First edition, December 2017

ISBN: 978-0-9991491-6-4

Library of Congress Control Number: 2017959874

Created in the United States of America

DEDICATION

This book is dedicated to my mother, who was also my very best friend in life. She was the kind of mother you could only hope to have — always patient, always providing and always loving. Her kindness and generosity earned her plenty of "surrogate children" wherever she went, but my sister and I were the two lucky ones who got to call her ours.

Mom — I miss our little getaway trips, our phone calls that lasted for hours and laughing with you until we both were crying. I wish I could've had you around for another 20 years, but I am so grateful for the 36 years that I did. And I promise to live out the rest of my years with a little more "oomph" just for you.

Until we meet again, I love you and I miss you.

– Your "Penelope Pitstop"

ACKNOWLEDGEMENTS

This book has been a LONG time coming. Even as I was living through the changes and the experiences described in this book, I had a notion that they weren't just for me. Yes, certain aspects of the journey were private and personal. But the overall themes and the life lessons I was being shown ... they needed to be shared and passed on to others. And I believe it is my responsibility to do just that — not only to fulfill my own purpose, but also to encourage others who may be struggling. I want to help them "take the blinders off" and live simpler and, hopefully, more joyful lives as well.

So, first off, I thank God for being patient with me as I dragged my feet for the past two years. And for lovingly, yet persistently, reminding me that I needed to write this book. And for bringing the right people and blessings I couldn't have imagined into my path. I am truly humbled and grateful.

Thank you to Cathy Fyock for believing in the power of my story and my book before it was ever even written. You have been a cheerleader, coach, teacher and sounding board all in one. I am so thankful that God brought us together in the way He did.

Kate Colbert, Courtney Hudson and the rest of the crew at Silver Tree Communications, THANK YOU for taking a chance on a first-time author like me and for gracing me with such a generous award. You have made my dream of reaching others with my story possible and, for that, I am eternally grateful.

Drew, MJ, Amy, Kari and Alexis, thank you for being my "guinea pigs" and giving me your honest opinions and feedback on this book. You were my very first readers (and always will be!) and I am so grateful for your help and kind words.

To the amazing, supportive, kind and super-cool members of the tiny house community, thank you for welcoming me into your world and for blessing me with some of the coolest friends I know. It truly is one of the most loving groups I have ever been a part of and I look forward to seeing you at many more festivals and events … hopefully with "Sweet Caroline 2.0" in tow!

Lisa, thank you for being my "healthy-living guru" and always being one step ahead of me and never too busy or bothered to educate your friend who was still one step behind you. Your guidance, advice and help kept me going when it all seemed overwhelming. And my body thanks you for it!

To my dream team, THANK YOU for being the first ones who finally made a difference in my health. For actually listening to me and hearing me. For helping me help myself and teaching me how to take control of my own health. You ladies rock.

Heather, my soul sister, thank you for being so supportive throughout this whole crazy book journey. I had no idea when I went to that writers' conference that I would be making a lifelong friend, but I am so grateful to God for you! I look forward to many more long phone calls as we continue on this journey together!

BB, my surrogate sister and BFF, thank you for being there with me through all of it. You had a front row seat to this whole journey and I honestly have no idea how I would've made it through without you. Love you.

And, of course … Mom, there aren't enough words in the world or space on a page to thank you for everything you've given me. So, I will just say thank you for ALWAYS believing in me, supporting me and loving me. And now, for being the inspiration behind my "new" life. I hope I've made you proud.

TABLE OF CONTENTS

INTRODUCTION

Over the course of just four years, I went through what could be described as an unusual amount of loss. In that short period of time, I lost:

- *My father (to stage IV cancer)*
- *My mother, who was also my BFF (to stage IV cancer)*
- *My dog, who I had for 14 years*
- *Two significant friendships (including my best friend since fourth grade)*
- *My engagement/relationship (which was also abusive)*
- *My job (which I had taken to escape a highly toxic work environment)*
- *My health (when I ended up with advanced adrenal fatigue)*

Needless to say, it was a lot to handle. But even more than the individual losses, I felt that I had lost something bigger — my sense of innocence.

Sure, they say you lose your innocence once you become an adult. But for me, it felt like that loss had come later. I looked back and suddenly realized I didn't even know how good I had it *when* I had it.

Things weren't perfect by far. But prior to 2009, I hadn't really had a significant loss other than my grandparents, who had passed away when I was fairly young. I hadn't yet been through the trauma of an abusive relationship. And, although I got sick a lot and had dealt with "stomach issues" since I was 20, I had otherwise enjoyed pretty good health.

It seemed like a simpler time ... one that I could only look back on in photographs, but never step foot in again.

Once that kind of loss takes place, there's no going back.

But the surprising part of my journey was instead of spiraling downward into a pit of despair, I did exactly the opposite.

Or should I say, God did exactly the opposite.

Even though I had quite literally been stripped of almost everything important in my life, I didn't fall apart. I didn't lie down. And I didn't give up.

No. Instead, God did what He does ... *made all things work together for good* (Romans 8:28) and used the string of hardships to strengthen me, to grow me and to draw me closer to Him.

And you want to hear something cool? God didn't just bring me through it. He allowed me to *triumph* over it.

Yes, I can actually say that I am more joyful, more peaceful and more content now than I have ever been.

So, how is that possible?

How can you lose almost everything in your life and come out joyous and victorious on the other side?

By getting back to basics and becoming the person that I was created to be. By getting rid of all the excess, all the noise, all the distractions and all the lies that I had been trapped in for years.

By letting go of attachments to things that didn't matter.

By looking at my body, my mind and my spirit in a new way.

By deciding to stop going through the motions and just surviving.

And *that* is when I actually started ***living***.

Chapter 1

THE GOOD OL' DAYS

I don't really remember when it started — my tendency to worry.
I feel like I just came out of the womb with a nervous stomach and
a furrowed brow.

That wouldn't be much of a surprise to anyone, seeing as my mother was
a gold-medal-level worrier and had probably been feeding her anxiety to
me through the umbilical cord for the entire nine months I was in the
womb. (Maybe *that's* why I stayed in there for an extra two weeks and
then came out weighing more than 10 pounds!)

I don't think my mom did it on purpose any more than I did. It was just
a learned way of life that we both picked up from our upbringing, as well
as the world around us. If you're warned enough times to "be careful"
on your way outside to play, you eventually learn the world must be
a dangerous place.

Not that life *inside* my house felt all that safe either.

Although I wasn't ever in any physical danger, my childhood was a bit of
an emotional roller coaster. My father was an angry person and, therefore,
yelled a *lot*. He'd yell at my mom, my sister and me for anything from

a phone call to a misplaced pen. Yet, there were other times when he could be funny and quite charming.

It was confusing for a child — to not know what kind of a mood your dad would be in and how he was going to act each day. But more than that, it was unnerving. It developed a habit in me early on to "walk on eggshells."

I'd tiptoe through my day, hoping not to do anything that would upset my dad, but still worrying that I might anyway. Or if I was able to get involved in playing a game or watching a show on television, I'd often be interrupted by the sound of yelling, so I learned to never get too comfortable.

Be prepared, so it never catches you off guard.

I also developed another habit back then that would carry through to my adulthood — the job of mediator.

Whenever my parents would argue or there would be uncomfortable tension in the house, I would take it upon myself to intervene. Whether that meant actually chiming in on the situation, doing something to distract them or just trying to change the feeling in the air by changing the subject, I would do whatever I could to "fix" it.

I got really good at nervous laughter, forced smiles and awkward transitions, even though they weren't usually all that effective.

I also became a bit of a perfectionist — wanting to do everything just right and desiring for everyone to like me. As the years went on, I'd be devastated if I didn't get along with a teacher or (gasp!) got a bad grade. In fact, the one time I got in any serious trouble in seventh grade, I felt like my world had ended.

I'm sure there was an underlying connection there … trying to be perfect and surrounded by happy people in all other areas of my life, because I couldn't quite control that at home. But in the end, it just added an additional layer of worry to my life.

Worry about grades, worry about friends, worry about teachers, worry about boys … you get the point.

But most of all, I worried about the people around me. I worried that my parents would get divorced, and I worried that they wouldn't. I worried about my dad getting to work safely every night because he worked the midnight shift. I worried about my sister when she moved away to college.

And most of all, I worried about my mom.

My mom and I had always been super close for as long as I can remember. Because my sister is six years older than me, she was already in elementary school by the time I came along and crashed the party. So, while she was at school, I spent my days watching soap operas with my mom and eating "rolly sandwiches," which consisted of slices of ham or bologna topped with a slice of cheese and, you guessed it, rolled into a log.

When I did go to school on the first day of kindergarten, I bawled my eyes out when I realized I was going to be separated from my mom for half the day. I got over it eventually, but I did still look forward to her helping out in the classroom or waiting for me at the bus stop when I got home.

And as the years went on, we remained pretty close. I never really went through that stage of rebellion where you hate your mother. There were times in middle school and high school when I kept things from

her as all teenagers do, but we never really had a falling out or any
serious disagreements.

All this made it all the more difficult when I moved to North Carolina
for college. Not only was I going to miss my mom, but I also felt a certain
level of responsibility for "protecting" her. Not from physical harm,
but from the emotional turmoil of living with my dad. I felt guilty for
leaving her alone.

But as I discovered the newfound freedom of college life, I became easily
distracted. I had a whole new world of friends, parties and boys to hold
my attention, and my mom had about 1,000 new things to worry about.

Plus, now that I wasn't living with my parents full time, the visits with
them were usually quite enjoyable. We'd eat meals out together, go shopping and tour the sites. But as much as I loved them, I was happy to be
able to go back to my own life after they left.

Things went pretty well for a while. I completed my Bachelor's degree,
got a great job straight out of college with a company car and corporate credit card, and started traveling on amazing business trips
around the country.

I also was making good money and had no credit card debt, which was
an accomplishment in itself seeing as I had racked up several thousand
dollars of debt in my years as a college student (that's what happens when
you find it necessary to buy a new little party dress to wear out to the
clubs every week).

I loved the financial freedom and lavished my family members with
extravagant gifts when I could, like sending my sister and her husband
on a weekend getaway, giving my dad a hang-gliding lesson and

sending my mom to a convention all about how to operate your own bed and breakfast.

See, even then, I was trying to help my parents reach their dreams and mark some things off their bucket lists. My dad had always wanted to hang glide and my mom always had a dream about owning and operating a B&B, so I wanted to give them both a head start.

My mom went to the convention and loved it, but never took action on a B&B. And my dad … well, like usual, he never even used the gift certificate for the lesson. It was pretty much to be expected on both parts, because I never knew either one of my parents to be risk takers or to step very far "out of the box." But even though I did grow up in that stay-in-your-lane kind of environment, the seeds of something more were starting to be sown.

I remember sitting at the kitchen table one day and making what I called a "life to-do" list. For all intents and purposes, it was a bucket list. But this was before the famous movie made bucket lists a *thing*. So, for me, it was a to-do list.

I threw all kinds of things on there … places I wanted to visit, lessons I wanted to take, things I wanted to do or participate in. There were about 50 items on there when all was said and done, but not one single thing got marked off for a long time. In fact, it wasn't until about six years later when I finally accomplished something on the list and it wasn't even a total match — I had "drive a race car" on the list and I actually ended up doing a ride-along. But I was so excited to actually do something remotely close to the list that I marked it off anyway.

The gifts to my parents and the life to-do list had sparked something in me.

I stayed in Frederick, Maryland, (where I grew up) for about two years
after my college graduation. Then after experiencing the terror of 9/11
first hand in Washington, D.C., I fled to my sister's house in Texas for
about six months. I know it was a bit of an overreaction, but I have
always been extra sensitive to things like that. I believe it's because
I have a strong sense of empathy and I feel things a lot more intensely
than some other people might. For instance, when the Batman movie
theater shooting happened, I stopped going to movies for a couple years.
I eventually made it back in a theater but spent the whole time visualizing what those people must have seen and felt that day, instead of
paying attention to what was on the screen. I haven't tried again since.

I didn't even really like working in D.C. anyway though, so once the idea
of random terror attacks became a reality, I wanted nothing to do with it.
But I also knew I didn't want to stay in Texas long term, so I eventually
returned to Maryland.

When I came back, I had another great job (outside the city) with a good
income and eventually moved into a beautiful two-bedroom condo about
15-30 minutes from all of my family and friends. My sister and her
husband soon moved back as well, which made me happy because I could
be closer to my nephew and my niece, who was on the way.

From all outside appearances, everything looked pretty good. But inside,
was a different story.

For one, I had been struggling with "stomach issues" since I was about
20. It seemed that no matter what I ate, my stomach would not be happy
with me and I'd always be running to the restroom after meals. Over
the years, I had developed anxiety about it ... not wanting to go out or

having to always know where all the restrooms were if I did. I didn't want to ride in cars with others or sit in the middle of a row at a movie or play because I needed to be in control of the situation "just in case." And it even got to the point where I didn't want to be in a quiet room like a meeting or a church service in case my stomach got upset and made loud gurgling noises.

But somewhere along the way, that anxiety had grown and started to completely take over my life. It wasn't just about my GI issues anymore … now I was petrified that I would do something — *anything* — that might bring the attention to me in a negative way. It wasn't just the chance that my intestines might cramp or grumble loudly, but maybe I'd break out into a coughing fit or, worse yet, maybe someone would call on me in a meeting or I *would* have to get up and use the restroom but I'd have to walk past a bunch of people to get there.

It was kind of crazy how fast the fear and anxiety multiplied until soon I wasn't doing much of anything outside of my house. When I would accept an invitation from a friend, I'd usually start getting anxious hours or even days beforehand and start to think about ways that I could get out of it. Most of the time, I would cancel. But if I did try to force myself to go, it usually wasn't much better. I'd purposely procrastinate and then end up running late and either miss the event altogether or just make my friend(s) angry.

I didn't like how my life was going, but I felt pretty much powerless to stop it. The more I thought about the anxiety, the more depressed I got. The depression played into the anxiety and vice versa. I started having full-blown panic attacks at work and at church. So much so, that I finally gave in and took advantage of my health benefits at work and began seeing a counselor.

She was a nice enough person and I think she meant well but, honestly, I didn't get much out of our weekly sessions other than an opportunity to vent. I didn't feel like things were getting any better and I was starting to think they never would.

Then one day, my mom told me that she had ordered a program for me that she had heard about on the radio. It was a self-study course that you did at home to overcome anxiety and depression. I don't really remember my exact reaction but I was so desperate that I was willing to try anything.

The program arrived a couple weeks later and it consisted of about 14 CDs and a workbook. Together, they helped you to attack the anxiety and depression from a behavioral perspective — by learning to recognize your thoughts and emotions, what triggered them and then, most importantly, learning to "re-train" your brain.

I dove into the program full force and would spend hours at home by myself listening to the CDs and scribbling in my workbook, while my friends were out living their lives. On one hand, it sucked. But on the other hand, it felt like the only way that I would ever be able to actually get back out there and live my own life again.

Because you were supposed to focus on one CD per week, it took me about three or four months to complete the whole program. But the crazy thing was, *it worked.*

Somewhere along the way, I had gained the strength to start doing things again. I started going to church again and was able to sit through the service without feeling the need to flee out the doors. I went on a road trip with a guy friend and shared hotel rooms with him (gasp!) and I even took a vacation with a friend and was able to get on a plane and a cruise ship. It was amazing!

I really, truly felt like I was free of that burden I had been carrying around. I was finally living again.

And that's when that seed from long ago popped up again. It was calling out to me … the life to-do list, the urge to break "out of the box," to do more …

I knew the time was right, so I decided I wasn't going to hold back. I was going to make a big move. Literally. So, without knowing a soul, I picked up my life and relocated to Charlotte, North Carolina.

Little did I know what was waiting up ahead.

Chapter 2

◆→————————→

THE PERFECT STORM

Moving to a new city where I didn't know a soul was both exciting and terrifying. I had never done anything like it in my life. I was always more of a homebody who stayed close to the familiar and who, like my parents, didn't step too far outside the box.

But I felt like I had reached a sort of plateau in my hometown. Most of my friends from high school were married and starting to live more family-centered lives with their husbands and babies. My job had unexpectedly been eliminated and the landlord who owned my condo had decided not to renew the lease because they were going to move back in. Plus, I did feel that desire in me again to "do more," to "see more" and, frankly, I was frustrated that I didn't have anyone with whom to do all of this "more."

So, I figured why not get a fresh start in a new place? And North Carolina had always been my second home. In fact, I used to joke, back when I was attending college in NC, that I had been born in the north by accident. North Carolina just always felt like home to me and when I left the state in the middle of my college career, I told everyone that I would be back. And here I was, staying true to my word.

In September of 2006, I packed up all my belongings and my parents helped me and my dog move into a rental house about 30 minutes north of Charlotte. It was in Lake Norman — a relaxed, resort-like lake town that had a wonderful way of making you feel like you were on vacation 24/7. It was still close enough to the city to pop in whenever I liked, but I didn't have to deal with some of the headaches of downtown living.

So for me, it was perfect. I remember how excited I was to have a brand new house that no one had rented yet (yes, the toilets were all new!) and how grown up I felt to have a screened-in porch, a garage and a driveway. My dog, Shauna, loved that she had a tiny backyard to roam around in and I loved that I didn't have to deal with noisy neighbors above or below me.

I didn't have a job yet, although it wasn't for lack of effort. I sent out plenty of resumes and had even taken a scouting trip to Charlotte with my mom weeks before I ever moved, where I went on several interviews. But unfortunately, nothing had really panned out except a part-time gig as an event assistant that I could work on an "as needed" basis. So, I immediately signed up with a few temp agencies in the city and started taking whatever jobs I could get.

I also had started to make friends on — of all things — MySpace. It was all the rage at the time and I have to admit looking back, it was a great way to make friends in a new town. I started going out pretty regularly with a few of them, doing the whole dancing and drinking thing.

It was fun and I was thoroughly enjoying my single life. That is, until my 30th birthday.

A guy who I only knew casually (because he had dated one of my MySpace friends) asked if he could join me and my friends at my birthday party. He had seen the announcement on my page and said he wanted to get out and make some new friends (he was no longer dating my sort-of friend). I figured he was nice enough (and kind of cute), so why not?

He ended up joining us for dinner where there was a bit of flirting between us, but then had to leave before we all went dancing because he had two young daughters at home and the babysitter was having a difficult time. So, we shared a hug in the parking lot and then I was on my way to the club with my friends.

In the car on the way there, my friend remarked that the guy (we'll call him Marshall) needed to find a nice girl, to which I gleefully responded, "I'm a nice girl!" and the stage was set.

The next day, an instant message from Marshall popped up on my computer screen. He had seen the birthday pictures I posted and apologized for not being able to hang out the rest of the night. We started chatting and before I knew it, we were making plans to go see the new Transformers movie the next night.

I was excited, but was trying not to make too big a deal of it. But when we ended up missing the movie altogether because we sat at the restaurant and talked too long (from like 7:00 p.m. until they closed at 2:00 a.m.), I was a goner.

Things moved very quickly in our relationship (which I later learned is a red flag) — we were official boyfriend/girlfriend status in about two weeks, said "I love you" in a month and he moved in with me at three months. Looking back, it seems crazy that I would even do something like that, seeing as I had always been super anxious about all the "boyfriend" things — meeting the parents, letting the guy see me without make-up, sharing a bathroom — but here I was, diving in headfirst!

I thought that was a good sign. And we actually appeared to both ourselves and others as "meant to be." We were ridiculously happy too, until slowly, I started to see signs of another side of him.

First, I caught him in several lies. Then, he started to make comments here and there to make me self-conscious. Then one day in the garage, he grabbed me by the arm HARD and spoke in a tone of voice I hadn't heard before.

Looking back, that moment in the garage was the first sign of abuse. But like I have told people many times before and I will continue to say, you CANNOT and DO NOT know what you would do in that type of situation unless you are in it. Of course, hindsight is 20/20. But at the time, I was just confused.

Remember, this was a person who I was already completely in love with by this point. I was invested in his family and his daughters. And did I mention that they were all living with me? So, although I was upset by it and we had a sit-down discussion about it, I eventually forgave him and we moved on.

Of course, you know the rest of the story ... unfortunately, over time, more and more of that side of his personality began to show. It wasn't all the time. In fact, that's what made it so confusing. There would be plenty of times where we still felt and acted like the most sickeningly sweet couple from a romantic movie. But sprinkled in would be nasty arguments, name calling, isolation and eventually physical abuse.

To say that it was a tumultuous time is an understatement. I walked around on eggshells most days, not knowing what kind of mood Marshall would be in. I so desperately wanted to just have my normal boyfriend — the one who I loved and adored — that I would do whatever I could to avoid an argument. Even if that meant not hanging out my friends anymore or doing things he didn't want me to do.

I didn't just ignore the abuse though. I told him that he HAD to do something about it. Originally, he agreed. He started seeing a counselor and began taking medication. But he quickly quit going to counseling and, unbeknownst to me at the time, began abusing the medication, along with other prescription pills.

I so desperately wanted to "save" him from himself that I tried and tried. Especially, because he would often sit and cry and pour his heart out about how he didn't want to be the way he was. But then he'd go right back to the same behaviors a day or two later.

Of course, I had also grown up in an environment that was very similar. In fact, I couldn't believe that out of all the men in the world, I had managed to pick such a carbon copy of my father (minus the physical abuse part). So, I was sort of raised unintentionally to be the co-dependent "fixer" type.

Eventually, we got engaged and the chaos continued for about two years until finally, one awful night in July 2009, it all came to a head.

I was leaving and Marshall knew it, so we were going to sit down to sort out the details of the lease and utilities before I left. Although he had originally reacted with somber sadness and remorse earlier in the evening, something inside of him flipped and he started taking it out on me. He drew a gun. I called the police, they took him away and he went to jail for a couple days. It almost doesn't even seem real as I write these words. But it definitely didn't seem real watching police surround my fiancé with raised weapons, demanding that he put his hands in the air.

However, that night was also the first night where I really *felt* God step in for me and take over.

Even though Marshall was doing awful things like pinning me down on the couch, shoving me around and pouring a can of soda over my head to humiliate me, I remained completely and eerily *calm*. In fact, I didn't even flinch when he poured the soda on me and instead, just sat perfectly still and asked him calmly, "Why are you doing this?"

Looking back, I know for sure that was the Holy Spirit giving me the strength and courage that I could not have on my own in such a traumatic moment.

After Marshall went to jail, I told my mother what happened and she and my dad came down to North Carolina immediately and moved me out of the house, despite my father being extremely weak with stage IV prostate cancer at the time.

I went back home with them in a daze, not knowing what I was going to do and not even really feeling very aware of anything. It's like I was just going through the motions of breathing, eating and sleeping. But I — the real me — wasn't there. My emotions were on overload between everything that had happened with Marshall, suddenly being back in my childhood home again and worst of all, watching my father quickly decline.

I made myself useful by helping my mother with my dad. But seeing your father reduced to a shriveled body who sleeps most of the day away and needs help to get to the restroom (or up off of the floor when he falls) is something you can never really prepare for. When he ended up going into hospice for just a half day and passing away that same night, a mere two weeks after I had gotten home, it was another huge blow.

I hadn't been very close with my father my whole life, but he was still my dad. And thankfully, we did have some sweet times toward the end that I will always be grateful for. But now, here I was, experiencing a MAJOR loss in my life. It was the likes of which I had never experienced before, and I felt like I was flailing.

I had lost the two most important men in my life (who just happened to be a lot alike) almost simultaneously. And I was living out of a suitcase in the spare bedroom of my parents' house, with no job, no fiancé, no direction and virtually no hope.

My mother had commented several times about how good I was with my father when he was sick, so we had started talking about the possibility of me going to nursing school. My mom offered to pay for my rent if I went to school full time; having no idea what else to do, I accepted. So against the wishes of my family and friends, I returned to Charlotte. I got a small one-bedroom apartment and a part-time job, and I started going to school.

But it wasn't long before I ended up going back to Marshall.

This is where a lot of people looking in from the outside may scratch their heads. *"Why in the world would you get back together with him??"* Well again, all I can say is, until you're in the position, you don't know what you would do. I certainly didn't.

Marshall had been my everything for two years. We were supposed to get married and live happily ever after. I was lonely and grieving. And of course, Marshall was back on his best behavior, claiming to have changed in every way.

For a while, things were okay. At first, we were giddy to be back together again. But slowly, the damage that had been done became apparent.

I couldn't ever fully trust him again and he could tell. He'd even made a comment about how he thought I was just staying with him until I felt strong enough to leave him. I guess in a way I was.

But as he started to feel me pulling away, the anger came back. There were more arguments, more names, more bruises and then, other women. Every time something would happen, I'd say that was it. And then, we'd end up back together again. It was dysfunctional, it was unhealthy and most of all, it was utterly EXHAUSTING.

I remember being on the phone one evening with Marshall while he talked about how awful he was and how he was planning to commit suicide and I didn't want to let him hang up. So, I sat in the same place on the floor in my apartment for hours — the sun set and night came, but I never got up to turn on a light. I didn't get up to make dinner for myself, or to feed or walk the dog. I was just there, on the floor, for hours.

After we finally hung up, I was actually scared for once that I didn't have the strength to make it. Not that I myself was going to commit suicide, but that I may literally die of exhaustion and heartbreak.

Thankfully, I did make it through and, in 2011, I finally stopped with all the back and forth and ended things with Marshall for good. I got more involved at my church, got baptized and even went on a mission trip. And as I prayed for God to silence both of us and keep us from reaching out to one another anymore, He answered my prayers.

Eventually, after a couple months, Marshall did begin to reach out to me again. He'd send emails and texts, call from different numbers and even post on my blog. But God had blessed me with just enough space and time that I was able to start healing and no longer felt compelled to respond.

I moved into a new apartment back at the lake, quit taking nursing classes (as I realized it wasn't the path for me) and got a great job in the hospital system with co-workers who I loved. Things were finally starting to be on the upswing and I was slowly starting to feel more like myself again.

So, I was surprised when I started experiencing a whole host of physical symptoms at the end of that year. It felt like my body was falling apart on me. And that surprised me, because other than some heart palpitations, I didn't really have any health issues while I was with Marshall and living at the height of stress every single day.

Yet here I was, finally starting to get things back on track and my body was virtually shutting down.

Just when I thought things were about to get better, they started to get worse. And I was about to find out there were more storms on the horizon.

Chapter 3

WHAT IS WRONG WITH ME?

By late 2011 and early 2012, I had racked up a whole list of symptoms that were affecting my body literally from head to toe:

- Headaches
- Dizzy spells
- Insomnia
- Severe allergies
- Muscle fatigue and pain
- Constipation
- Stomach pain
- Shakiness
- Hypoglycemia
- Cystic acne
- Heart palpitations
- Shortness of breath
- Anxiety attacks
- Brain fog/difficulty concentrating *(including one very scary morning where I literally couldn't figure out how to get on the highway, even though I was accustomed to taking the exact same exit every day).*

I changed jobs in January of 2012, and began working a regular shift (as opposed to second or third shift at my previous job) at a doctor's office, which proved to be increasingly difficult as my symptoms worsened. Most days, I barely had the energy to get out of bed when my alarm would go off at 6:30 a.m., so I'd drag myself into the shower and usually leave the house with wet hair and no make-up. Luckily, I didn't work with the public directly, but I started getting "marks" on my record because I was constantly clocking in late.

I also was under a lot of stress in my new position because I worked in a small room with no windows and dealt with extremely strict rules about everything from how long I could be away from my desk to how many pictures I could put up. I also received a lot of inappropriate remarks from my co-workers on a daily basis. I tried to just stay quiet and stick to my corner of the room, but the stress definitely wasn't helping my health.

Because I was working in a doctor's office though, I took advantage of my health benefits once again and started to see physician after physician to find out what was wrong with me. I saw a primary care physician, a gynecologist, an endocrinologist, two gastroenterologists and a cardiologist … all to be told the same thing — there was nothing wrong with me.

It was beyond frustrating.

Knowing that something is wrong with your body, feeling like it is literally shutting down on you, yet being told everything is "normal." The gastroenterologists put me on several prescription medications that made me feel worse. They sent me for a colonoscopy, a barium enema, X-rays and CT scans, and even had me take a pill that contained small rings so they could do an X-ray shortly after and watch how the rings passed through my body. And yet again, the doctors all said everything looked fine.

Several of them did offer one "solution" though — anti-anxiety medication or antidepressants. It was infuriating. Not only were they denying my symptoms, but they were basically telling me that I was imagining them and that I needed to be medicated.

After breaking down in tears on the exam table one day in a doctor's office, I had had enough. I was done with "traditional" medicine. I knew there had to be another way, so I started looking into naturopathic doctors in the area.

I found one online who had a lot of great reviews, so I made an appointment with him shortly after. I knew that I wouldn't be able to use my insurance coverage for "non-traditional" medicine, but I was desperate.

The very first appointment that I had with him made any extra cost worthwhile.

After my initial consultation and blood work, he was immediately able to not only confirm all the symptoms I had been having, but also tie them together with direct correlations between one another.

I wasn't crazy after all!

The verdict was finally in. I had adrenal fatigue and a pretty severe case of "leaky gut syndrome" (a condition where the lining of your gut has holes in it, which allows bad things to get into your bloodstream and good things to get out). Together, these conditions can wreak total havoc on your body.

My new doctor immediately started me on a very strict diet called the Repairvite diet. I couldn't have any grains, dairy, sugar, alcohol, caffeine, condiments, eggs, nuts, seeds, nightshades (like tomatoes and peppers) or processed/canned foods. Basically, I *could* have organic vegetables, low-glycemic fruits and antibiotic-free, hormone-free, grass-fed meats. That's it.

The whole point was to give my GI tract a break from anything that could in any way be irritating or inflammatory, so it could heal. I also drank water mixed with a Repairvite powder (which was a mix of herbs and vitamins) several times a day. This would help to repair the lining as well.

He also put me on several supplements for my adrenals, thyroid, blood sugar and concentration, and then sent me on my way with a hefty bill.

It may have been pricy and it may have sounded a little crazy to outsiders, but the results were well worth it. Within just a couple weeks, I began sleeping soundly through the night without any medication and my skin clearly up completely. I also started going to the bathroom normally again (which after months of not doing so, was enough reason to celebrate!).

Even the shakiness, that I for years had thought was "just me," stopped altogether. Turns out, the tremors and the low blood sugar attacks (hypo-glycemia) were not something that I was just born with, but rather my body's reaction to the roller coaster I was putting it on with all the sugar in my diet, my poor eating habits and the long periods of time I would go between meals.

We were making progress, although I was a little frustrated that he seemed to be addressing my issues slowly and individually, instead of working on an "overall" cause. Things were still much better than they had previously been, and I was happy to finally have someone who knew what they were talking about, so I continued the diet for a whopping SIX months!

When the six months were finally up, we began to slowly add a restricted food or ingredient to my diet, one at a time, so I would be able to tell if my body had a reaction. It seemed that my body was still pretty intolerant to dairy and gluten, so I cut them out altogether and tried to stay as sugar-free as possible as well, to keep my blood sugar in check.

Things were going pretty well and again, I was starting be hopeful that I was about to "turn a corner" when another storm came blowing in. And it was a big one.

My mother, who had always had some digestive issues due to her nerves (like me), had recently begun to have more difficulty. Because she lived so far away in Maryland, we had only talked about it by phone and she told me that she had also begun seeing a naturopathic doctor who put her on some dietary restrictions of her own.

Because I was having such a positive experience with my naturopath, I was happy to hear that she was going to one too. But I also strongly encouraged her to go to a "traditional" doctor as well, just to make sure that everything was okay.

See, my mother had a bit of a phobia about doctors and hadn't been to one the entire time I was alive.

Yes, 30-some years and my mother had never been to the doctor once! Or the dentist for that matter (although she somehow still had good teeth). It was a sore subject for both me and my sister, who would periodically beg her to go, only to eventually give up after her half-hearted promises to follow through, until the next time, when we'd do it all over again.

As we had gotten older, my sister would tug on our mom's heart strings by saying she needed her to go so she could be around for her grandchildren to grow up. And I would do the same by telling her I needed her at my wedding one day. Those attempts usually had a little more of an effect on her than when we just talked about the benefits for her, because my mother was the type who always put others before herself.

But even our best efforts to "guilt trip" her into going usually failed.

In September of 2012, my mom came down to North Carolina so we could go on a Labor Day trip together to the beach. We often did trips like this together because I was still single and my mom was alone (and we were BFFs).

But when I saw her for the first time at my front door, my heart dropped.

Just looking at her, I could tell that she had lost weight. A LOT of weight. In fact, to be honest, her facial structure reminded me of how my dad looked when he was sick, which scared me. When I commented on it, she just brushed it aside and said it was a result of the restricted diet. I questioned the accuracy of that because I was on a restricted diet too but hadn't lost a substantial amount of weight. But I let the issue go for the time being and we left on our trip.

While we were away though, I noticed my mother having more severe symptoms like barely making it to the bathroom, not having as much strength/energy as usual and having discomfort sitting down (which she blamed on hemorrhoids).

I continued to bug her to go to a regular doctor and have a complete medical workup, just to be sure everything was okay. And again, like always, she promised she would.

A short time after that trip, I was back home at my apartment, working on a project for a client, when I had what I can only call a burst of intuition. I have always had a very strong intuition, especially when it comes to those who are close to me.

Once, when I was living in Maryland, my mother and I had been Christmas shopping together at a mall near my apartment. When we went to say goodbye in the parking lot, I had a very uneasy feeling about leaving her. I figured it was just my anxiety acting up, so I ignored it and got in the car. But as we pulled out of the mall, I looked in my rearview mirror just to make sure I saw her pull out. She did and I continued to watch her for a few moments, as I went up the long hill toward the highway. After glancing down for just a few seconds though, I looked up again and noticed that I couldn't see her headlights anymore, which I thought was odd because it was a straight hill without any exits.

I couldn't shake the uneasy feeling, so I was relieved when my cell phone rang on the passenger seat just about five or ten minutes later and the screen said "Mom." I picked it up, ready to chit chat and make that weird feeling go away, except that she wasn't on the line. I could hear her speaking, but she was talking to someone else, a man, and I heard her say "I just the hit the ice and it went over." The man, who I could then tell was a police officer, said something that I couldn't quite understand, but my heart jumped. I kept calling out that I was on the line, but she couldn't hear me. So, I immediately made a U-turn and started heading back to the mall.

She still didn't know that her phone had "accidentally" dialed my number until I got all the way back to the scene and nearly slid into the police officer myself. When she got in the car to go back to my apartment with me (her car was on its roof), I told her about the eerie feeling I had right before it happened and we both were in awe.

So here I was again, sitting at the computer working on a freelance project regarding the Farrah Fawcett Foundation. I had no prior knowledge of it, but as I sat there reading about anal cancer, I had this overwhelming feeling that I needed to call my mother and bug her again to go to the doctor. It was something I had done a million times already, but something about that article gave me a fear in my gut that I knew something that I didn't want to know.

I called her and gave her the usual routine of begging and pleading and tried to casually mention the Farrah Fawcett article without freaking her out. And as usual, she promised she would go see a doctor.

The holidays came and went, and by the end of January, my sister and I both felt like we were hearing less and less from our mother, which was VERY strange for her. Historically, my mom and I would talk multiple times a day and once had stayed on the phone for six hours straight! Granted, it was from like 7:30 in the evening until like 1:30 in the morning, but still … we talked for the length of some people's workday!

So, my sister and her husband finally went out to her house one day and found out the truth. My mother wasn't doing quite as well as she was trying to make us believe and had actually stopped doing much of anything but taking her pain medication and lying in bed. She had stopped doing laundry, the Christmas decorations were still up, there was moldy food in the refrigerator and she had even stopped taking her dog outside.

It was bad.

My mother had never, ever been the type to neglect anything. She was the role model of a good mom — making the meals, doing the dishes, doing the laundry, taking care of the home. After my father passed away, she had redone their whole bedroom and bathroom in pale blues with ocean scenes on the wall and inspirational books on the bookshelf. She always did her hair in the mornings, wore makeup and dressed in cute outfits.

This was not our mother.

My sister called me and told me what was going on and said she was going to move our mom in to their guest bedroom at their house in Virginia, which I thought was a great idea. She also said my mother had an appointment to finally go see a doctor about the severe hemorrhoids and the incontinence. My mom wasn't thrilled about seeing a doctor, but she was finally in so much pain and discomfort (and obviously depressed), that she gave in.

Except that when she *did* go see the doctor in March of 2013, the news wasn't what any of us expected to hear. It wasn't hemorrhoids after all.

My mother had stage IV anal cancer.

Chapter 4

❥➺━━━━━━━━━●➤

DARKEST BEFORE THE DAWN

I remember exactly where I was when I got the news, as I imagine most people do when they get that kind of news about themselves or a loved one. (Side note: Unfortunately, I don't have one of these "moments" for my dad, because in the typical fashion of my parents, I don't even know how long my dad had cancer before I found out and I honestly don't even remember how or when I did. For one, I was in the middle of my tumultuous, abusive relationship. But also, it was the kind of thing that we just *didn't talk about*.)

I was sitting in a steakhouse having dinner with a friend of mine. My sister had assumed that I had already heard the news from my mother and called to see how I was handling it. But, she quickly found out that I didn't know yet, based on my reaction.

I remember looking at my dinner through teary eyes and telling my friend that we needed to get the check. And I remember wandering aimlessly through a housewares store after that. My friend was trying to figure out what to say to someone who had just received that type of news and I was trying to just comprehend what I had found out.

During the next couple of weeks, I went back and forth about whether or not I should move back to Maryland. My mom was still going to be living with my sister at her house, but I felt like I should be closer. Being six hours away in North Carolina seemed too far.

Of course, my mother, who adamantly put everyone else ahead of herself, refused to have me move. She kept telling me how my life was established in North Carolina and that by me *not* living there, it made it all the more special when I did come up.

I called bull crap on that one, but I still went along with her wishes.

The good thing was, God — in his perfect and divine plans — had already set me up to be able to visit a lot. In December, before we had even found out about my mom, I had finally gotten out of the dungeon job at the doctor's office and got my first full-time writing job. As the newest reporter in the newsroom of a local paper, I had thought that I was finally living out my purpose. I didn't love the small town location or the fact that I had a 90-minute commute each way, but I thought for sure, I was where I was supposed to be.

That is, until I was let go after only one month.

I had never been let go from a job in my life. So, when the publisher of the paper called me into her office and I saw the rep from HR sitting there, I didn't even take that as a hint. I literally didn't know what was going on until she began speaking and told me that it "wasn't going to work out" and that they were letting me go — exactly 30 days after I had started.

I was flabbergasted and had called my mom in tears on the way home. I was totally confused and didn't understand why, when I finally was in a job that made some sense, it was being taken away.

But, that was at the end of January. The next month, I started working as a personal assistant for a local entrepreneur who was in the health and wellness industry. Not only did she focus on a lot of the same things I was learning about with diet, supplements and meditation, but I was also able to work a flexible schedule, often working from either her home or mine.

When my mother was diagnosed in March, it all began to make sense.

Had I stayed at the newspaper job, I would never have been able to travel back and forth to Virginia to see my mom. But now, with a flexible schedule, I was able to visit her as often as I wanted and work from my sister's house while I was there.

For the first few months, my mom seemed to be doing really well. She was basically having zero side effects from the chemo — she never lost her hair, didn't have trouble eating and never got sick. The thing that she did struggle with the most was the colostomy bag that she had to get right after her diagnosis. I know it was embarrassing and frustrating for her, but we all tried to help her deal with it the best we could.

Toward the middle of the summer though, my mom began to show more signs of the disease — her hair got thinner, she lost a lot of strength and, eventually, had to walk with a walker. It's strange how your brain adjusts rather quickly to seeing and experiencing these types of things; I'm sure it's a defense mechanism to get you through the moment. But now, thinking back, I'm a little surprised at how well we adjusted.

By the grace of God.

At the end of August, my mom and I were scheduled to have a two-week vacation together. It was going to be a week of her staying with me in Charlotte, followed by another one of our trips to the beach.

It became obvious pretty quickly though that this wasn't going to be one of our usual trips. She had gotten very weak since I had last seen her and she began to fall — repeatedly. *That* was probably the hardest part of the whole process for me. I don't think you ever really get over seeing your parent lying on the ground, unable to get up.

We still managed to get to the beach and had a pretty nice time, despite the circumstances. But by the time the end of the week rolled around, she didn't want to get out of bed because she was feeling so weak. Assuming she needed another blood transfusion (something else we had just gotten "used to"), we decided to head back early and get her in at the hospital in Charlotte for the transfusion.

Thankfully, they were able to get her in, give her the transfusion and keep her overnight. My sister and her husband drove down with their kids to pick her up and drive her home and by the time I saw her the next morning, she was looking more energetic. I felt a little better, although that intuition of mine kicked in again as she was getting in my sister's minivan to leave.

My mom casually smiled and waved at me from the front seat as I walked away and I had a strong feeling that that was the last time I was going to see her like that.

I didn't know what it meant and I tried to ignore the fact that I'd even had such a thought, but it was there nonetheless.

For the next week, I tried to ignore that feeling of doom and tried repeatedly to call or text my mom, but hardly heard back from her at all. This, again, was *very* out of the ordinary for her.

I also was having a dreadful feeling about her birthday that was coming up that Saturday, but was trying my best to write that off as anxiety as well.

But when I sat down in the chair at my hair salon on Saturday morning and got a call from my sister, my dreadful feeling was confirmed — my mother had been unresponsive when my sister went to wake her.

You never really can prepare yourself to hear words like that. And having seen the same thing happen firsthand with my father, I knew what that meant.

I, of course, jumped in the car and headed up there as fast as I could. When I got there, my mom was awake (she had actually gained consciousness in the ambulance after my sister called 911) and under a bunch of blankets in the ICU. They told us that she had a very low body temperature and that she was anemic and undernourished (she had been driving my sister and me crazy with not eating enough). So, we took that to mean that we just had to be better about getting her to eat.

But, as the days began to pass, I started to have more of that clarity that I didn't want to have. I started to realize that even though I had just begun making plans to move up to Maryland right before I got the call from my sister, I didn't think I was going to need to move.

Somehow, I just knew that my mother wasn't going to be leaving the hospital.

It was during this time that I again felt the very real presence of God, and Him holding me up with His strength, as opposed to my own. In fact, my sister even unknowingly recognized it and commented on it one evening as we walked the halls of the hospital.

"You're taking this a lot better than I thought you would," she said.

It was a bit of a back-handed compliment, but I knew exactly what she was talking about. Not only was I able to handle my mother being extremely ill and weak, but I was also staying by her side every night, talking to doctors, talking to my sister, reassuring my mom and basically functioning a lot better than even I would've expected.

By the grace of God.

My mother did end up leaving the hospital after six days and immediately went into hospice care at my sister's house. Because Mom had always wanted to live at the beach and had even talked about having Thanksgiving that year at the beach, my sister had redone the guest room while my mom was in the hospital and covered the whole thing in pictures of the ocean, put an ocean-themed comforter on the bed and even put on a sound machine with the sound of seagulls.

There are some difficult memories of things that I saw and heard during that next 24 hours, but when my mother passed away the next night, my sister and I were both right by her side.

The Lord had held me up every day while I was in the hospital, sleeping in an armchair by the side of my mother's bed. He had held me up while I was taking care of her at my house and at the beach. He was keeping me strong for all the difficult things I was seeing and hearing. But when she took her last breath, I finally let go and all the tears flowed out of me like a river.

On one hand, I was blessed because God had used the experience with my father to prepare me for my mother's passing. I was much closer to my mother and may not have been able to handle everything if I didn't already know what to expect. But having already been through the hospice and death experience with my father, I already knew the order of how things happen … how they look, how they act, everything. So not only was I already prepared for it, but I was able to advise my sister as well.

I also had a supernatural form of peace about me during those weeks leading up to her passing because I knew that whatever happened, God's will would be done. It's hard for some people, particularly non-believers, to understand that. But I knew that God was in control no matter what. Obviously, I wanted my mother to get better and I wanted her with me here for many more years to come — so she could see me get married, see me have kids and all the other things I wanted to share with her still.

But, I also knew that if it was time for God to call her home, that He would get me through. And I wanted her to know that I would be okay too. So I told her that a few hours before she passed. She was back to being unresponsive by then. But they say your hearing is the last sense to go, so I know she wanted to know that I would be alright without her and I believe that gave her peace.

The next two weeks were a blur with me writing my mom's obituary, being interviewed for an article about her for the local paper, and planning and attending her memorial. My sister's neighbors were kind enough to bring us dinners every day, most of which were well off of my healthy eating regimen, but I didn't much care.

I hadn't given up necessarily. But I was focusing all of my energy on just getting through the day, so everything I had been doing to pay attention to my own health had basically gone out the window. I was having gluten, dairy and sugar again. I wasn't sleeping like I should be and I stopped taking supplements or seeing my naturopathic doctor entirely.

When I did get back to North Carolina, I had another stressor to deal with — moving. Because I had given my 30-day notice just prior to my sister's phone call (so I could move up to Maryland and be closer to my mom), my landlord had already re-rented my house. So now, on top of everything else, I had to move.

Luckily, I found a two-bedroom apartment close by and sort of mindlessly moved in a few weeks later. I had a small amount of money from my mother's life insurance that helped with the moving expenses and security deposit. And although I had returned to my assistant job for a couple of weeks, I was having trouble keeping up with the commute and the demand of my employer's schedule, so I quit and took a new job working at a dog kennel close to my apartment.

I had always been extremely passionate about animals, particularly dogs, and was already boarding dogs in my home part time as a way to supplement my income, so I figured this job would help me to stay upbeat.

I started seeing my naturopath again and slowly began to get back on track with my diet and my supplements. But even though I was starting to take care of myself physically again, emotionally, I was slipping.

I think I knew that I was sort of just "floating" along, going through the motions of living every day. But it wasn't until I attempted to go on a date just two months after my mom's passing that I realized how bad things were getting.

The guy had done one of the whole presto-chango moves where he went from expressing his undying affection during the date to disappearing off the face of the earth immediately after. But it wasn't even him that shook me. It was how I felt afterward.

I remember clearly thinking, *"Yea ... yea ... I know. I'm strong, I can get through this. But you know what? I am TIRED of having to be strong. I am tired of having to get through things. I don't know how much more I can take."*

During this time, I was still a believer and I never got angry with God. In fact, to this day, I still never have. I did honestly have peace about His will. But you can have peace about His will and still have grief, sorrow and lots of other heavy emotions that eventually will take a toll on your body and your mind.

And as I was about to find out ... on your spirit too.

After I had those thoughts that night, I started to notice that I was acting a bit out of character.

I would spend endless hours just zoning out in television or YouTube videos. I found myself tempted to "hook up" with a guy who was much younger than me. And I even emailed an old guy friend of mine who was now married, that I had no business contacting (not my finest moment).

They were all things that I normally wouldn't do and I just didn't feel "right." Even though I had been a Christian since I was 27 years old, I had never really given much thought to the reality of Satan, temptation and evil forces. Which is kind of silly when you think about it, because if you believe in God and His power to do right in the world, it only makes sense that the opposite exists too.

But it was like all of a sudden, I realized that I was under spiritual attack.

Now, I know this may be the part where some of you may be feeling a little uncomfortable ... but stick with me. Just because you haven't thought about something before doesn't mean it might not exist. Plus, I felt the exact same way!

I had no idea what to do about it really other than to ask for prayer, but I was a little embarrassed and unsure how to even ask for it. So, I reached out to my friend, who also happened to be in charge of benevolence at our church and she came right over.

Thankfully, she didn't look at me like I had three heads, and she promised to pray for me. So did a couple of other close friends.

And the cool thing is … once you realize that Satan is trying to do his whole "steal, kill and destroy" thing and you ask God for help, he instantly flees the scene.

❧————————➤

Submit yourselves, then, to God. Resist the devil, and he will flee from you.

– James 4:7 (NIV) –

Thankfully, after I recognized what was happening, faced it and prayed for God to help me, that's exactly what He did.

Even though I still struggled with real emotions like grief and anxiety, and my body was still not operating as it should be, I did have more peace in my spirit.

I stopped losing hours and days in mindless activities, I blew off the younger guy. And the married friend didn't respond. Thank God.

I also had a bit of an epiphany one night while looking through some of my mother's books, which I had brought back with me after her memorial.

I was sitting on the floor of my guest bedroom, flipping through her journals and taking in as much of her handwriting as I could because it made me feel like she was near. And I came upon one entry that really struck me. My mother (who was probably about 66 or 67 when she wrote this) had said that she had let fear hold her back from doing so many of the things she wanted to do in life. That she had lots of ideas and dreams, but that she had been too afraid to go after most of them.

It absolutely broke my heart and made me feel sick to my stomach. It wasn't just because she had no idea at the time that she would pass away just six years later. But also, that she had run out of time to do the things that she kept talking about, like living in a house at the beach and driving a VW Beetle convertible.

It was in that very moment that I decided I was going to live *differently*.

I didn't want to end up like my mother, realizing in my late 60s that I had let fear hold me back from living. But, I also didn't want to run out of time. My mother had no idea how long she had and neither did I.

I was already so much like my mother that I could easily see myself going down the same path. I was like her in so many ways — some good and some bad. I worried a lot, I tended to play things safe, I was ridiculously empathic about other people and I had even replicated her relationship with my dad in my relationship with my ex.

There I was in my early 30s, with advanced adrenal fatigue, constantly worried or anxious, with mounds of debt and working a job that had nothing to do with what I knew to be my life's purpose — writing.

Something needed to change.

Both for me and for her.

Chapter 5

STRIPPING ME DOWN

Gardeners prune trees to help them grow.

Pruning can make a tree's roots stronger, making it more able to withstand storms. Removing dead limbs or branches also prevents infection and disease in the tree and produces healthy fruit. From the outside, it also makes the tree more beautiful, because all the dead areas are removed and what's left is healthy and alive.

I didn't realize it at the time, but 2014 was the beginning of my pruning season.

On the surface, I thought I had already been pretty "pruned." I had lost my relationship, an important friendship, my parents, my health and — from how it felt most days — my joy.

But that was actually just the beginning of the process.

By that spring, I was in a new place in my life. Both literally and figuratively.

I had moved in with a new roommate — a friend I had met at the dog park, who quickly became my best friend and surrogate older sister. Inspired by my mother's journal entry and determined not to let fear control my life, I had also quit my job at the kennel and committed to doing my writing full time.

It was a huge leap of faith that I felt was almost immediately confirmed, as I began to pick up new freelancing assignments from local magazines and individual clients around the world. Because I was unable to do in-home dog boarding anymore with my new roommate, I had also picked up several regular dog-walking clients who I visited four to five days a week.

I was starting to feel a little better physically, so I stopped seeing the naturopath and decided that I was going to dive headfirst into my new life's mission of being unafraid and not waiting to live.

I even had a name for it: my **GOBHPPY** mission.

The name had come to me in a dream (or perhaps, more accurately, a message from my mom). One night, while I was still living by myself at my apartment, I had a nightmare about my mom. In it, we were standing side-by-side at some sort of church service, when all of a the sudden, the most purely *evil*-sounding voice I had ever heard whispered something in my ear. I couldn't tell what it said, but it was so close to my ear, that it sent chills down my spine.

At the same time the voice whispered in my ear, my mother fell to the floor next to me. I looked at the person who had been standing on the other side of her, and she was staring back at me with wide eyes and an open mouth. We immediately tended to my mom, who thankfully was okay (in the dream) and then I woke up abruptly.

Needless to say, I was a little freaked out and felt like there was an evil presence in my room. So, in my half-asleep, half-awake state, I said to myself, "Think something good about mom."

Instantly, a complete image popped into my head. It was a beach scene, with the ocean to my right and, up to the left, a beach house on a hill. In front of me was a green VW Beetle convertible parked facing away from me, with a license plate that read "GOBHPPY."

Immediately, I knew that this was a message from my mother to **GO BE HAPPY**. She had wanted to live in a beach house and drive a green Beetle convertible and she had run out of time. So, she was making sure to remind me to go be happy right now, while I could.

I had jumped out of bed that night to write it all down before I forgot. And I made a commitment to do just that — go be happy and start marking things off of my old "life to-do list" as quickly as I could.

Although I hadn't made a lot of progress on it just yet, I had taken one pretty major step that was *way* out of my comfort zone.

I scheduled myself a trip to Europe that fall. It was through a tour company, but I would still, for all intents and purposes, be by myself, seeing all the sites of Europe that I always wanted to see.

Pretty good way to start off the bucket list mission! Right?

I had changed the background image on my laptop to a beach scene that said "Life is too short to wait" and I was determined to get out there and start living an amazing life that my mom would be proud of.

But, God had other plans for me.

Inspired and motivated by my new life's mission, I was keeping pretty busy. I was walking dogs five days a week, working on my freelance writing gigs and going out regularly with friends. I had even Googled "exercises for people with adrenal fatigue" so I could get moving again without causing further damage, as I was still very easily fatigued.

The only problem was that, even though I was mentally ready to live a life full of adventure and fearlessness, my physical condition was a different story.

As the weeks and months went on, I noticed myself getting more and more fatigued on my daily dog walks, to the point where I could barely make it through a 10-minute walk with my last client. I was also feeling heart palpitations on a regular basis every day. I was becoming exhausted from taking a shower and felt like I might have a heart attack just from carrying my laundry across the house.

I kept trying to ignore it. I was supposed to be "not waiting to live," after all! But my body was screaming out to me every chance it could get.

I was educating myself on adrenal fatigue as much as I could … devouring books on it left and right, with one particular book, *Adrenal Fatigue: The 21st Century Stress Syndrome* by James Wilson, becoming like a second Bible to me.

Although my naturopathic doctor had never given me a formal diagnosis of adrenal fatigue, he had mentioned that there were adrenal issues going on, which were causing a lot of my other symptoms. As I sat and read the book by Wilson, I felt like it could've been titled *This is What is Wrong with You, Jenn Baxter.*

Not only was it a dead-on description of all my symptoms, but I realized through reading that book that I was dangerously close to stage IV adrenal fatigue, which is where you are basically bedridden.

I covered the book in little Post-It flags, marking pages about what to eat, what supplements to take and other lifestyle changes to make.

I purchased special skin care products for adrenal fatigue to help with my extremely dry skin and ordered yoga DVDs and a CD of breathing exercises that were made particularly for those struggling with adrenal fatigue.

But when I suffered a major adrenal crash after attempting to do a simple breathing exercise from the CD, I knew I needed help.

In September of 2014, I reached out to a neuromuscular therapist (NMT) in Charlotte. I had found her website while searching for exercises for people with adrenal fatigue. As a "survivor" of AF herself, she was now working with children and adults, helping them to reintegrate their reflexes through tapping and bodywork (I didn't really know what that meant exactly but it sounded interesting enough to inquire).

I sent her an email explaining my situation and asked if she might be able to help me. And to my overwhelming relief, she said yes.

I made an appointment to see her, as well as a new naturopathic doctor closer to my house. This doctor was a woman who attends my church and came by high recommendation from a friend. Although most of the basic techniques and therapies were similar, I was much more excited about this doctor because she incorporated spiritual and emotional health into her treatments.

After my initial hour and a half appointment with her, we had a game plan in place (a BIG one) that included a healthy diet, LOTS of supplements and a few other treatments, including an infrared sauna and electromagnetic therapy.

When I went to see the NMT, she quickly diagnosed a lot of my natural reflexes as being out of whack. Basically, we all have certain reflexes that help us to survive life. For example, the Moro reflex, which is the reaction to a sudden, unexpected noise or the fear of being dropped. Or the Freeze reflex, which literally paralyzes your body in response to a danger that your body feels it can neither "fight" nor "flee."

Turns out, your reflexes can get overused and become overly sensitive from a host of different things (usually traumas). Of course, I was not surprised to hear that my body was shooting off these primitive reflexes in an attempt to "survive." After being through almost four straight years of significant traumas, I'm surprised they were functioning at all!

The NMT also referred me to an occupational therapist (OT) who she herself had been to and often worked with. She was a counselor of sorts — but not in a typical way. She helped patients address the root causes of issues and deal with them through meditation. Again, I was more than happy to give it a try, seeing as everything else had failed at that point!

And just like that, I had found my "dream team."

I call them my dream team because, having run into dead end after dead end with traditional doctors, these three ladies made the biggest difference in my health in the shortest amount of time and I am forever grateful to them (and to God for bringing them into my life).

Although I had to quit my regular dog-walking jobs because it was too much strain on my body, the silver lining was that I suddenly had more time to focus on my health.

Thankfully, I still had some of my inheritance from my mother, as well as my writing jobs to keep me afloat. I was also blessed that I didn't have to get up at a certain time or fight with a commute and instead, was able to stay in bed and sleep in if I needed to.

And there were definitely days when I needed to.

Simple things like taking a shower or carrying laundry would still exhaust me. Sometimes the fatigue would be so intense that I would be nauseated and would have to immediately lie down. I had to be extremely careful about eating every four hours and make sure to consume plenty of protein, or my blood sugar would quickly dive, causing another crash. Most days, I would also get in bed by 10:00 p.m. and not rise until 9:00 a.m.

The important thing though, was that it was *working*.

Yes, I would still have bad days and I was nowhere near "normal." But for the first time since all of this started, I was finally starting to see light at the end of the tunnel. Each time I would go back to the naturopath, the NMT or the OT, we would see *progress*. And progress meant I was at least moving forward, not backward.

My social life had pretty much come to a halt and the whole "bucket list mission" unfortunately had to take a backseat, including my beloved trip to Europe. It was a tough proverbial pill to swallow; my entire life perspective had become all about not waiting and yet here I was literally being forced to WAIT.

But it was quite clear where my focus and energy needed to be and that was on my health. If I didn't get that straightened out, I wouldn't be able to do anything off the bucket list anyway.

So, I buckled down and began a steady routine of healthy eating, taking supplements, using the sauna and electromagnetic treatments, doing meditation and seeing the NMT.

Luckily (because my insurance didn't cover natural health treatments … *don't get me started*), I was still able to keep up with my overnight pet sitting as another source of income.

In fact, it was during one of those overnight sits earlier that summer that a new obsession was born. And it was one that was about to come into play BIG TIME.

I was staying at a friend's house watching her dog and two cats when I made a discovery that would pretty much change the course of my life.

They didn't have cable television, so I had resigned myself to the couch one night with a blanket, the dog and Netflix, and began scrolling through the programs to see if anything caught my eye. I somehow ended up in the documentaries section and noticed a movie called "Tiny."

The description said *"Two young people decide to downsize their lives by building a 'tiny home' on a flatbed trailer."*

I had absolutely zero clue what a "tiny home" was, but it sounded interesting enough, so I decided to give it a go.

Over the course of the next two hours, I was mesmerized. And by the end of the movie, my heart was racing.

THIS was what I needed to do.

Here I was trying to live this new kind of life ... I had never been much into possessions or having too much stuff anyway ... and I had been planning on using the small amount of money that my mom had left me to put a down payment on a condo or a townhouse. But now, I could outright build and own a house for the same price and be truly rent- and mortgage-free!

I could barely sleep that night, excited to get started on this new path for my life. My mom didn't leave me a lot of money, but with a tiny house, I could set myself up to have almost NO monthly expenses. I had purchased my car outright, paid off all of my credit cards and now would own my home as well.

I knew my mother would be proud and so excited for me.

So, I immediately began diving into all things tiny house. I recorded and watched every episode of Tiny House Nation. I pinned hundreds of pictures and design ideas on Pinterest. I read books and took e-courses. And I started making plans for my own tiny house.

I was determined that this was not going to just be something else that I started and didn't finish. Or something that I just talked about but never actually did. That was a bad habit and an echo of my mom's regret. So, this time, things were going to be different.

I created a wishlist of *"must haves"* for my house — things like:

- Plenty of headroom in the loft (I am a tall girl, after all!)
- An actual staircase instead of a ladder
- A comfortable couch that I could actually relax on
- A functional kitchen (meaning a dishwasher, stove/oven and a fridge that did NOT fit under a countertop)
- A washer/dryer combo

- An outdoor space like a little front porch or a deck

And I also started researching builders. At the time, tiny houses were a "thing" but they weren't exactly a "big thing" yet, so there weren't nearly as many builders as there are today.

Luckily, North Carolina (particularly the Asheville area) was a bit of a hub for the movement, so I had a few options close by.

I started to schedule phone consultations with builders and mainly asked fairly simple questions about the dimensions of the homes, prices, delivery dates and, of course, if they would be able to accommodate my wish list.

Looking back, I now know I should have been asking a LOT more than that.

My budget was only $30,000, and I was finding that a lot of the builders were out of my price range. Most of the small homes started at $40,000 if not more, and even though I wanted a tiny home, I didn't want a *tiny* home. I at least wanted something larger than 100 square feet!

By October, I had found a builder in Tennessee that I was really excited about. They built a home that I frequently drooled over on Pinterest and I just loved the overall look of their designs — lots of clean lines, white walls, dark wood accents and functional living spaces.

I reached out to them and, after an initial phone consultation, we began discussing details by email. I knew I would have to settle for a smaller home (probably around 120 square feet) to work with them, but I was more interested in having a beautiful home than a big one.

Plus, the whole point was to go tiny, right?

The process of getting a final quote turned out to take a lot longer than I had expected, so I had to try to be patient, while the builder and I went back and forth with emails for the next two months.

By the time Christmas rolled around, I still didn't have a final number and I was starting to feel like this builder wasn't the one for me after all. I mean if it was this hard just to get them to nail down a number, what would my build process with them be like?

On New Year's Eve, they finally got a final quote over to me and, much to my dismay, it was nearly $10,000 over my budget.

That pretty much sealed the deal on them and I begrudgingly accepted the fact that I was going to be starting my search all over again. That is, until I opened my email the very next day.

I had received a message from another builder I had inquired with months before, who had told me at the time that he wasn't ready for a new build because he was in the process of moving his business from the coast to Raleigh, NC. But now, he said, he was all settled in, ready for a new build and wondering if I was still interested in doing a consultation.

I couldn't believe the timing! I had a good feeling that maybe this was "meant to be," so I called him right away and we discussed all of my needs, wants and my budget and we seemed to click on everything. At some point in our conversation, we also bonded over our faith as he shared that he and his wife had been praying for the right first customer and I told him that I had been praying for the right builder.

Yes, you did read that right. His *first* customer.

I was aware that he had only built one house up to that point (which he used as a model home), but I really liked the way it looked and, honestly, I believed that this was divinely designed. He, being a new builder, would be more willing to work with my small budget, and I, being a freelance writer and blogger could give him free publicity for his new business. I also had just heard back from HGTV about a show I applied to be on, called *Tiny House Big Living*, and they had decided to cast me and document my tiny house experience, so he would be getting even more exposure on television.

It seemed like a win-win.

So again, I started the process of emailing back and forth, going over all of the details of my tiny house on wheels (THOW).

There were SO many questions … what type of roof material to use, what shape the kitchen should be, what type of countertop material to use. There were so many things I had never even thought about and had no real knowledge of, so I pretty much played it by ear as I went along.

Again, looking back, I can see how I let the excitement of my new adventure get ahead of some important planning and research. But I also figured that if I were going to buy a traditional home, I wouldn't have to educate myself on how to build it. That is the builder's job. And that is why I was choosing to have a home built, as opposed to trying to do it myself.

So, I trusted that the builder would know what he was doing. And as we moved forward and I signed a contract for him to build my home, I focused my attention on the more interesting parts, like the design and — of course — the downsizing.

If I was going to be moving into a 160-square-foot tiny house, I had to get rid of some stuff. A LOT of stuff. The last time I had moved, into my roommate's house, I had filled up a 17-foot U-Haul truck by myself.

I remember standing on the curb, looking into the back of the truck as the movers pulled the door down, surveying the piles that reached from the floor all the way to the ceiling, thinking ...

"How in the world does one person have so much stuff?"

Chapter 6

DE-CLUTTERING THE PHYSICAL JUNK

Once I had signed on the dotted line and made the tiny house dream an official reality, I knew I had to get to work. One of the biggest draws of tiny living for me was owning only the actual necessities and nothing more, so I was excited to get started.

I was also slightly overwhelmed.

The way things were set up in my roommate's house, my belongings were kind of spread out. I had my bedroom furniture and clothes in my bedroom, my extra bedroom furniture in her guest room, my toiletries and towels in her guest bathroom, and all my living room furniture and desk/workspace were upstairs in her bonus room. All the other stuff that I wasn't currently using (like my kitchenwares, mementos, books, holiday stuff, etc.) was in her garage. I also had a few random things in her attic.

Like I said … spread out.

But I knew the tiny house would take about four to five months to complete, so I had some time. I decided to start working on the small things first. Luckily, I've been a very organized person since I was little, so this process was going to be orderly and efficient.

→→ ————————→ *F.A.S.T.* TIP ←———————— ←←

Work on reviewing your possessions by dividing them into groups or small chunks.

I began making my way through my life's belongings one "group" at a time. That way, I wouldn't get too overwhelmed and I would hopefully stay on track and not bounce from room to room. A lot of times, this is where people get hung up on organizing or going through clutter. Altogether, it can seem like an endless amount of stuff that you can't possibly get through. But broken down into manageable chunks, it seems much more doable.

I started with things that felt simpler to me, like the bedroom, living room and kitchen, and left the more complicated stuff, like my mementos and decorations, for later. If I did find something that belonged in another space or I had questions about it, I would simply set it aside for later and keep working where I was. This kept me on track and kept me from getting distracted.

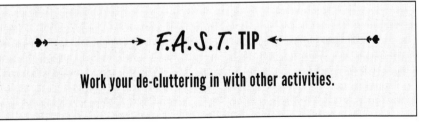

→→ ————————→ *F.A.S.T.* TIP ←———————— ←←

Work your de-cluttering in with other activities.

I would also work the downsizing into my schedule by combining it with other activities. For example, I'd go through the clothes in my closet when it was time to put laundry away. Or I would sit down and go through my movies and CDs while I watched TV.

My overall mindset while going through my stuff was one of ruthless honesty. For one, I was only going to have 160 square feet in my new home (which included very minimal storage). But also, I was done with having so much *stuff*.

I genuinely wanted to downsize to only what was absolutely necessary, by either usefulness or importance, and get rid of all the excess.

Some of it was pretty easy. I knew the time had come to get rid of my VCR and VHS movies (although, my father would've been proud that I had kept them for so long). I also easily let go of a LOT of books and kept only those that I had read and *knew* I would rely upon for reference or read again, and those that I hadn't read but genuinely intended on reading. The ones that had been hanging around for years, just gathering dust, had to go.

This was the first part of the de-cluttering process where I realized I could start making some of my money back.

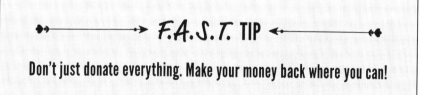

◆▸ ──────▸ F.A.S.T. TIP ◂────── ◂◆

Don't just donate everything. Make your money back where you can!

Instead of just dropping off my movies, CDs and video games to the local Goodwill store, I decided to take them to several used bookstores in my area. The process went like this — you'd drop off your items to a "buyer" who would review them while you browsed around the store or waited patiently with your vanilla latte at their on-site coffee shop. They would determine if it was something they wanted to sell, if it was in good condition, etc. and then after about 15-20 minutes, would offer you cash for the items they decided to keep.

Usually, it was only a few dollars for each book. So, I never walked out of the stores with a pocket full of Benjamins. But I always left with more than I went in with, which for me was a *score*.

It was also pretty easy for me to let go of my second bed set because I had owned it for years and wouldn't be needing one bed frame in my tiny house, much less two. I sold it on Craigslist, along with the small television that I previously kept in my guest bedroom.

The closet was surprisingly easy to tackle, although the process of going through my clothes, shoes and accessories was quite surprising.

Generally speaking, I didn't think I had a lot of clothes. I consider myself to be a fashionable person, but I've never really been a shopaholic or cared much about designer labels. If anything, my mom had taught me to appreciate a good bargain. Plus, I felt like I had just gone through my clothes fairly recently and pulled out a lot to donate, so I figured most of the work was already done.

Boy, was I wrong.

It is CRAZY how your closet can act as a bit of a black hole, swallowing up mounds and mounds of clothing without you ever even noticing. Seriously, for a little while, I was beginning to wonder if I had one of those rotating closets like Cher in the movie "Clueless," because it just wouldn't end!

Again, being the OCD organizer that I am, I decided I was going to use a process to go through my clothes. It would be too hard to just randomly pick things out here and there, so I decided to go through my clothes in three separate sweeps:

1. First, I went through my whole closet and pulled out anything that had holes, tears, or stains, and those items that were worn out, faded or otherwise damaged. Those pieces of clothing were pretty easy to get rid of.

2. Then, I went through the closet again and concentrated only on pulling things out that were no longer appropriate — things that were too small for me, too young for me or even a few things that were too old for me. This is where I realized that I held on to clothes for WAY too long, because I could actually recall memories of wearing certain items more than 10 years ago. I also got rid of my "worst case scenario" clothes during this sweep, which for me, meant business attire. Although I hadn't worked at a job that required formal business attire for years, I still had a whole section of my closet that consisted of blazers, dress pants and suits that were quickly gathering dust. Not only did I not have a need for them anymore, but this was also a pivotal moment for me because I realized that by deciding to get rid of them at this moment, I was *committing* to myself that I would never again work in that type of job. Of course, I know that you can't ever 100% predict the future, but what I was doing in that moment was making a promise to myself that I would commit to living the kind of life that I wanted to live, which did not include that kind of job. So, I would be sure to make all my future decisions based on that promise. Bye-bye, suits!

3. Then, after everything was gone that was damaged, didn't fit or wasn't age-appropriate, I was left with all only garments that were technically salvageable. There was no particular *reason* for any of these remaining items to go, which is why this sweep came down to SELF-CONTROL and HONESTY. Now, it was time to really face the facts and ask myself what I *actually* wanted out of what was left and what was just going to continue hanging in my closet for years to come without ever seeing the light of day. It's estimated that most people only wear about 20 percent of their wardrobe (isn't that crazy?) and I was no different. As I went through everything this last time, I had plenty of those *"Awww ... I forgot I had this!"* moments, BUT I didn't let myself fall for the nostalgia. If I hadn't worn it up to this point, there was a reason, so I wasn't going to keep it.

I told you ... ruthless.

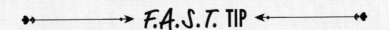

→ F.A.S.T. TIP ←

Don't just donate all of your clothes to the most common or obvious organizations either — look for other options in your community, like domestic abuse shelters, homeless shelters and programs that help people who need professional clothing for job interviews. Or make some of your money back by consigning your gently-used items.

At the end of the closet massacre, I had SEVEN trash bags full of clothes, shoes and accessories that were going to the domestic abuse shelter, a pile of business clothes to donate to Dress for Success and another small pile of clothes to sell at a local consignment store.

In the kitchen, I got rid of several "one hit wonders" — appliances that only serve one very unique and specific purpose, like a waffle iron and a dog bone maker, both of which I never touched. I also downsized my coffee mug collection, which had somehow multiplied up into the double digits; I kept just four or five of my favorites, mostly ones with sentimental meaning attached.

The bathroom was fairly easy as well — just a matter of throwing away expired medications and vitamins, tossing half-empty bottles of products and finally admitting that I was never going to get around to using those hot rollers or that foot spa.

But just when I thought this whole de-cluttering and downsizing process was going to be a piece of cake, I hit a bit of a road bump.

After spending a few weeks going through everything inside the house, I decided it was time to go through some of the stored items in the garage. It was time to look through my holiday decorations, photos and mementos.

And as the kids today like to say ... that's when stuff "got real."

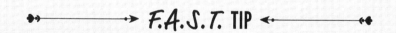

F.A.S.T. TIP

When going through your mementos and items with sentimental value or memories attached, don't try to do too much at once. Take your time, take breaks, and give yourself time and permission to feel any and all emotions that may come up.

If you're going to do a downsizing and de-cluttering process of your own and take only one piece of advice away from this whole book, let it be that one right there.

Being the Tasmanian Devil that I am when it comes to organizing and purging, I decided to do almost all of my keepsake stuff in one fell swoop. And when I say "all," I mean SIX large Rubbermaid bins and a massive steamer trunk full of mementos. What can I say? I'm a sentimental person.

Yes, in one single sitting, I was going through family photos, souvenirs, notes from school, yearbooks, baby clothes, greeting cards and scrapbooks. I was looking at pictures of my mom, my dad, dogs who had passed away, and photos of my niece and nephew when they were little.

Any ONE of those things could make a person tear up a little. Yet, I decided it would be a grand idea to go through all of it back-to-back.

Didn't turn out so well.

After I came in from three or four hours in the garage going through everything, I got in the shower. While I was standing there, I felt like I had something stuck in my chest — like I had to cough really hard or something. Yeah, turns out that "thing" was grief.

And it all came pouring out about 30 minutes later.

Thankfully, my roomie/BFF was there to listen to me vent about everything and even she commented on how I may want to take it a little easier next time.

Ah yes, hindsight is always 20/20.

But, there was a good side to it as well. In fact, it became abundantly clear to me that night that this whole downsizing thing wasn't just about making space and getting rid of the excess physical stuff.

It was about getting rid of some *emotional baggage* too. And the timing was in no way coincidental.

I very well knew that a big part of healing my body (particularly my adrenals) was to release a lot of repressed emotions that had gotten stuffed down inside over the years. That is, after all, what stressed my adrenals to the point of exhaustion in the first place.

But I hadn't realized that the downsizing/de-cluttering process was going to help me do that until that night.

As I looked at pictures of loved ones who had passed away, friendships that had ended, my niece and nephew as children, and myself as a child, I was forced to confront the emotions that these items brought up.

And for the first time in a long time (if ever), I let myself *feel* them.

When the bubble started to rumble up from my chest, I didn't push it back down. I let it come up. And even as I continued to go through more mementos after that night, I decided to really *sit* in it and let myself feel the process.

I'm not going to sugar coat it … there are times when it's really tough. But in the end, it is all more than worth it, because it allows you to finally heal a lot of old wounds. Which in turn, lets you release the items because they're no longer entangled in old emotions.

As I did the emotional work that I needed to do (more on this later), I was able to really make progress on the de-cluttering. I narrowed ALL of the mementos — even the contents of the massive steamer trunk — down to just two small bins that would fit perfectly on my THOW's secondary loft.

I got rid of my prom gown, my graduation gown and my high school pom uniform because, seriously, even though they were kind of fun to look at, when was I *really* going to use them again? I got rid of all my yearbooks except for my senior year and when it came to the holiday decorations I had inherited from my mom, I kept only the ones that I actually liked or that had a particularly sentimental meaning. Which, did NOT include the creepy, giant Styrofoam Santa head that used to hang in the living room (sorry, Mom and Dad).

The real challenge, though, came when it was time to go through the photographs.

I hadn't really realized that there was a bit of a taboo related to throwing away photos until I started to do it. It seriously felt *weird*. Like I was going to look up and see a patrol car in the driveway and an officer walking into the garage saying, *"Ma'am, I'm going to need you to put down those photographs."*

But the moment I had an epiphany that I didn't actually *have* to keep all of them was when I was flipping through an album from the cross-country trip my family took when I was 10 years old. It was an amazing month-long trip and something very out-of-character for my family, so it was something I will always remember.

But when I was going through the album, I realized that about 80 percent of the photos were of random trees or rocks or streams. I'm sure when I was snapping away with my 110 Le Clic camera, I was well aware of what each one was. But now, 20 years later, they all looked the same to me.

And it was then that I realized it was actually *okay* to get rid of them.

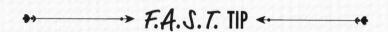

F.A.S.T. TIP

Even though it feels somehow wrong, or even illegal, to throw photos away, I promise you, you can do it. Especially if they are just photos of random scenery or landscapes. Feel free to shred, recycle or trash!

Of course, I kept the pictures of me and my family, or particularly impressive shots of sites like Mt. Rushmore or Devil's Tower. But all the other randomness, including the 100 or so pictures of antique cars that I took at some random museum in Illinois, ... yeah, those went in the trash.

I also had inherited a lot of old family photos from my mom and dad, which I went through and separated into two categories — ones that I just wanted to be able to look at and ones that I wanted to actually have physical copies of. The latter I put in a fireproof safe, along with some of my important documents.

Then I took the others, as well as a few of my old VHS tapes, and set them aside to be transferred onto DVD. That way, I would still be able to view them whenever I wanted, but I didn't have to keep the original photos or movies.

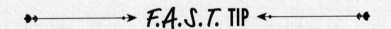

◆◆ ─────────→ F.A.S.T. TIP ◄•──────── •◄

Transfer old photographs onto DVD and add titles & music to make a keepsake that you will actually enjoy viewing and will take up less space!

There was one other hidden lesson that I learned while going through my physical clutter — to be present with who I am *now*. This meant letting go of a few ideas, like:

- The person I used to be.
- The person I thought I "could" be *one* day.
- The person I thought I "should" be.
- The person other people wanted me to be.

A lot of the things that we tend to hang on to often fall into one of these categories. Maybe you're keeping clothes you used to fit into or supplies for a hobby that you always wanted to take up but never did. For me, it was a tennis racket and a yoga mat that I used to move from place to place, even though I hadn't played tennis since high school and I had never gotten around to starting yoga.

Or maybe you're holding on to things that represent a version of yourself that you felt pressured by others to become. For example, if your mother was a jewelry maker and her mother before her, so you've kept a room full of supplies, except that you have zero interest in it whatsoever. We often hold on to these types of items simply out of a sense of misplaced guilt or responsibility.

For me, I didn't so much have a role that I felt obligated to fill for others, but I did have some clutter that represented roles I had put myself into. For instance, when I downsized, I had a rolling craft cart that was FULL of all kinds of supplies for scrapbooking, candy making, soap making, latch hook and needlepoint. Yet, I hadn't really sat down to do any crafts since 2003.

I had held on to them for so long because I thought I would pick it back up "one day." But I also felt like I *should* be a crafty person. A lot of my friends did crafts and I loved pinning pictures of cute projects I wanted to try on Pinterest. It's just that they never seemed to get done. And given the choice between crafting and doing something else, the something else always won out.

So, this time, as I went through my stuff with my new ruthless attitude, it was time to be honest. If I hadn't played tennis, started yoga or become Martha Stewart by now, chances were, it wasn't going to happen. And that was okay.

I could let go of those items or, in the case of the craft cart, pass them on to someone else who would actually use them, and focus my time and energy on things that I *did* enjoy doing instead.

In fact, that seemed to be the BIG lesson that I learned going through all my belongings and eventually getting rid of about 80 percent of them — that by doing so, I was getting down to just the basics. The things that I *do* use, *do* need, *do* want and *do* enjoy.

It also gave me a bit of a reality check as to how mindlessly I had been living up to that point. I'd become "blind" to a lot of the things around me and wasn't focusing enough on the things that do bring me joy.

But now, things were about to change. And as I felt myself getting lighter and feeling freer as I let go of physical clutter, I became even more motivated to keep going.

Now it was time to clean up my body.

Chapter 7

CLEANING UP MY BODY (ON THE INSIDE)

When I was diagnosed with adrenal fatigue, I started paying more attention to my health than I ever had in my life.

It's not that I was like my mom and totally ignored it up to that point. If anything, my sister and I had inherited her worrying, which manifested as hypochondria for us both. We'd obsess over every little bruise and bump and pretty much do what everyone else does — go to the doctor for relief.

But after my disappointing and extremely frustrating experience with "traditional" doctors (not to mention what I learned about traditional medicine and cancer when my mother was diagnosed), I began to pay attention to my health in a *different* way.

Instead of just mindlessly going to the doctor and taking whatever they said as gospel, I began to educate myself. After all, I had run into so many dead ends with them by that point that I really became disillusioned with the idea of traditional medicine as a whole.

I felt like God was "stripping me down" so clearly — pulling away all the clutter, the noise and the distractions and getting me back to the core of who He had created me to be. And this was no different.

I was starting to look at my body and my health from a more spiritual and natural standpoint.

It only made sense — as the proverbial blinders were being taken off about materialism, possessions and the American dream, I felt like I was being "woken up" about my body too.

Here we all are, mindlessly consuming toxic ingredients in the foods we eat every day, not to mention slathering them on our bodies and around our homes, yet we are all so shocked and saddened by how rampant cancer has become.

[Note: I do not mean to offend anyone with what I say here. I, too, have had many family members pass away from cancer. So my intention is not to be harsh or disrespectful. But it IS to be blunt.]

The truth is that most of us (including me right up until this time) either don't bother to pay attention or don't want to pay attention to the truth about our food and products. We cover our eyes and put our fingers in our ears, and then hope that if we are ever "unlucky" enough to get cancer, that a pill or toxic treatment will save us.

Seems a little backward, doesn't it?

Why *wouldn't* our focus be on doing whatever we can to prevent disease in the first place?

Why *wouldn't* we intend to live the healthiest lives that we can so we don't have to fight disease later?

And why in the world *wouldn't* we want to be educated on the things that we are putting in and on our bodies and our loved ones' bodies?

Sure, it's easier to just avoid the truth. To write it off as fiction or conspiracy. Or to ignore it *"just this one time"* so we can indulge in something decadent.

But once you've had your own personal health crisis or watched a loved one go through one, it becomes a little more difficult to ignore.

I wanted to know what was really in the foods I was eating and the products I was using every day. And I wanted to make changes that would not only help heal my adrenals, but help me to live a purer, cleaner life (to go along with my tinier, freer lifestyle).

So, I started doing research — reading books and blogs, taking courses, talking to my dream team and even farmers at my local farmer's market.

Some of what I found was obvious — organic fruits and veggies are obviously healthier because they aren't sprayed with pesticides, drinking plenty of water is important and eating small meals throughout the day will help keep your blood sugar level.

But what I *wasn't* really prepared for — what I guess I was pretty naïve about myself — was just how much we don't know.

Even in our modern, democratic country, there is a LOT that we don't know that's going on behind the scenes in our food industry and our healthcare industry.

Now, don't worry, this isn't going to turn into a conspiracy theory book at this point. But I DO want to shake you up a little and get you to pay attention!

The truth is, we CAN'T just walk into any old grocery store and buy a food item off the shelf or walk in and purchase a body care product from any old drug store and assume that it's safe to use or consume just because it made it to the shelves.

Because that is NOT the case.

I won't get into all of the nitty gritty details here. But I will suggest the documentary, "Food Inc." if you want to get a good idea of just what's going on behind the scenes in the food industry. *(Be prepared though ... whether you've ever considered being a vegetarian or not before, you may want to become one after watching!)*

Many, and I do mean *many*, of our foods today are pumped full of all kinds of toxic ingredients — antibiotics, chemicals, artificial flavors, colors, dyes, preservatives and hormones. *(Ever wondered why kids are developing so much faster these days than they used to?)*

There are entire labs with staffs of scientists whose job it is to chemically "create" foods ... to genetically modify them and alter them with God-knows-what ingredients. *(Ever wondered how a potato chip can taste like garlic bread or a jellybean can taste like peanut butter and jelly?)*

We drink fluorescent blue beverages, eat fast food that contains petroleum and anti-foaming agents *(I'll refrain from saying where from)*, and use cosmetics with cyanide in them and then we wonder why we all get sick.

It all was enough to shake me to my core. And I knew I was ready to make some changes. BIG ones.

❧━━━━━━━━━━❧

GLUTEN

The first thing I did to clean up my diet was to remove gluten. I had already started eating gluten-free when I was on the restricted diet from the first naturopath that I saw back in 2011. So, when I started to really focus on my diet after my adrenal fatigue diagnosis, it wasn't like I had to start completely from scratch.

If you're not even sure what gluten is or what all the fuss is about, let me give you the basic rundown. First of all, gluten is not wheat. Yes, it is *in* wheat. But it is not the same thing as wheat. *(I cannot tell you how many times I've been in restaurants with uneducated servers where they try to assure me that something is safe for me to eat because it doesn't have wheat in it. No way … there's no wheat in salad dressing? Go figure.)*

Gluten actually refers to certain proteins that are found in wheat, as well as other grains like rye and barley. Basically, it acts as "glue" (hence the name) and holds foods together. This is why it's so important not to make the mistake about wheat, because it is indeed found in many products that you might not think of right away. In addition to the obvious culprits like bread, baked goods and pasta, gluten can be found in things like:

- Soup
- Salad dressing and marinades
- Sauces and gravies
- Condiments
- Luncheon meats
- Protein bars
- French fries (especially at restaurants!)
- Soy sauce
- Candy

- Cereal
- Potato chips
- Beer
- Medicines
- Cosmetics
- Shampoo
- Even the glue on pre-moistened envelopes!

The other thing that you probably have heard of by now is *Celiac disease*. Celiac disease is a serious autoimmune disorder where an allergic response to gluten causes the body to attack the small intestine. In the short term, it can cause uncomfortable symptoms, like severe stomach upset, diarrhea or vomiting. But left unchecked in the long term, it can lead to other autoimmune disorders, neurological conditions, skin issues and even cancer.

Fortunately, I tested negative for Celiac. However, because of the adrenal fatigue, my body had developed a sensitivity to gluten. I actually think I had an intolerance for it for years, seeing as I had been dealing with "IBS" (a catch-all diagnosis they give you when they can't find anything else that is wrong) since I was about 20 years old.

When I ate foods containing gluten, my stomach would get upset, usually resulting in me running to the restroom. But little did I know, over time, those episodes with gluten (and other inflammatory foods) had actually formed holes in the lining of my gut. It's what's referred to as "leaky gut syndrome." This is why the first naturopath that I saw put me on the Repairvite diet — to *repair* my gut.

Although the restricted diet seemed to have done its job and created some relief, I knew that me and gluten were done for good. I dove into being gluten-free 100% and I haven't looked back since!

(Now, I'm not going to lie … there have been times when I snuck a piece of bread or a bite of a cupcake here and there over the years, but trust me … it's never worth it in the end.)

Going gluten-free actually wasn't (and isn't) as hard as many people think. Or even as difficult as I thought when I first decided to make the change.

It can seem extremely overwhelming at first, not only having to go through your cabinets and know what to pull out, but also knowing what to replace it with and more importantly, what ingredients you're supposed to be looking for in the first place.

There *will* be a bit of an adjustment period. But I promise you, it is definitely worth it and it gets a lot easier pretty quickly. In fact, it comes so naturally to me now that I can't even remember a time when it seemed challenging!

Basically, when it comes to ingredients, you just have to know what to look for. Again, don't just look for "wheat." There are lots of other names that gluten can hide under on an ingredient label. Ideally, you want to look for a "gluten-free" label on your foods and beverages. But, in the case that something is not labeled, keep your eyes out for these ingredients to ***avoid***:

- Wheat (including durum, semolina, spelt, wheatberry, graham, farro, einkorn, emmer, wheat starch and hydrolyzed wheat protein or HWP)
- Barley

- Rye
- Malt or malt flavoring
- Brewer's Yeast

And when in doubt, don't be afraid to ask!

I used to be the kind of person who was afraid to speak up or cause any trouble, so I wouldn't ask questions when I was in a restaurant or store. But once I decided to take control of my health, that went out the window!

The only way I was going to make sure that I remained healthy was for me to stay on top of things. I couldn't depend on the waitress who thinks all salad dressings are gluten-free. *(In fact, the few times that I did doubt a server's expertise and chose not to speak up, I always ended up regretting it later.)*

Don't be afraid to ask your server in a restaurant, or even better, ask for the manager or the chef. Most times, they are more than happy to oblige (to avoid problems later) and will happily give you the information you are seeking. The same goes with stores, whether they're brick-and-mortar or online. Don't be afraid to ask the manager about a product or give the support line a call.

Fortunately for you and me, there are also plenty of wonderful bloggers out there who have compiled gluten-free menus from popular restaurant chains for easy reference. So, even if you're already at the restaurant, don't be afraid to tell your server to give you a few minutes while you pull out your phone at the table and do a little research. Restaurant websites and apps like Find Me Gluten Free also tend to be more reliable when it comes to nutrition and allergen information than a restaurant employee.

It's better to be safe than sorry. Especially, if you have a gluten sensitivity.

So, of course, the magic question then is … what if you don't have a sensitivity? Should you still avoid gluten?

In my humble opinion — I say, *yes*.

Because when it comes down to it, gluten isn't exactly good for any of us. Even if you don't have a sensitivity to gluten now, you can develop one at any time. *(After all, I didn't until I was in my 30s!)* But beyond that, gluten can cause a whole host of trouble even for those without an actual allergic reaction.

Gluten is inflammatory to the gut, period.

Over time, this can result in gastrointestinal permeability (or holes in the gut), just like it did with me. Those holes let toxins escape from your gut and get into your bloodstream, where they can then travel all over your entire body and wreak havoc. This is why someone with severe migraine headaches or a skin condition can find relief when they cut gluten out of their diet — the root cause was the gluten that caused the holes --→ which allowed the toxins to escape --→ which caused the inflammation in ____ part of the body.

Damage caused by gluten can lead to other autoimmune conditions as well, like diabetes, rheumatoid arthritis and even dementia and Alzheimer's Disease. On a smaller scale, it can cause short-term GI disruptions, like diarrhea, gas, bloating and heartburn, as well as skin rashes, insomnia and brain fog or difficulty concentrating.

So really, why would you choose to subject your body to this?

Now, if you're sitting there on the other end of this book, screaming at me, *"Because I love bread!,"* it's okay. Breathe. I love bread too. And the good news is that you can find alternatives that are actually delicious. I promise!

First of all, if you're the domestic type, you can make all sorts of tasty breads, cookies, brownies, cakes and other baked goods at home using gluten-free flours like:

- Almond flour or meal (my favorite)
- Coconut flour
- Tapioca flour
- Chickpea flour
- Oat flour
- Rice flour

There are other options as well, but these are the most common. You will also find that some of the big names in the baking industry have now begun selling gluten-free flours or gluten-free flour mixes that are an easy one-to-one conversion for traditional flour. If you do not use one of these types of flour, just be sure to check the conversion rate, so you know how much to use. For example, almond flour will deliver a much different consistency from coconut flour. Usually, the conversion is listed right on the package for easy reference.

If you're not the baking type, there are lots of ready-to-eat or ready-to-heat gluten-free options available in the stores too. You can typically find gluten-free bread, muffins, pizza crusts, waffles, pancakes, cupcakes, cookies and crackers pre-packaged in your local grocery store. Of course, these items won't be as natural as something you would make at home (because of preservatives and other additives) and they tend to be high in sugar and sodium, but they're okay to have on occasion.

Although I do purchase gluten-free bread from the store (Canyon Bakehouse is the best!) and the occasional cookie or cracker, I do prefer to make a lot of my baked goods at home. That way, I know exactly what is going into my food and I can control things like sugar and GMOs *(we'll get into both of those in just a bit)*.

It will take a little while and some trial-and-error to find what you like best, but the results in the end are well worth it.

In fact, I can usually tell pretty quickly if I do accidentally eat something with gluten in it or ingest it unintentionally, because my stomach will get mad at me. But, I also will feel fuller, lethargic and even a little spacey. *(Ever wonder why all you want to do is take a nap after a big pasta dinner?)*

These days, I am more than happy to oblige my body. The better things you put in it, the better results you'll get out of it!

LEARN MORE

Check out some of my favorite gluten-free items and recipes on my blog at *www.LiveaFastLife.com* or through my "De-Tox" course at *www.DeClutterDeToxDeStress.com*.

DAIRY

The next thing that I cut from my diet when I went clean was dairy. I wasn't much of a dairy person anyway; in fact, I hadn't actually had a glass of milk since I was a little girl. But I did love me some cheese and ice cream, so it was going to be a little challenging for me to let those go.

Again, I had a head-start on this from doing the restricted diet for six months. My body had pretty much been detoxed of dairy during that time, which had also allowed my brain to let go of some of those obsessive thoughts *(particularly over the ice cream)*.

Plus, I already knew my body didn't really handle dairy all that well from when I was younger. Pretty much whenever I would eat ice cream or have too much cheese, my stomach would get loud and gurgly. I'd feel like the Goodyear blimp and couldn't wait for it to digest so I could feel normal again. *(Yet, that wouldn't keep me from going back again. Ahh ... humans.)*

This is actually a pretty common reaction for people to have. In fact, most adults *can't* process dairy (or more accurately, the sugar *lactose* that's in dairy products). When we're young, our bodies produce an enzyme called lactase that digests the lactose. But, that enzyme usually stops being produced between the ages of two and five. Meaning, the undigested sugar ends up fermenting in the colon instead, where it produces gas, cramping, nausea, diarrhea and other blimp-like symptoms.

It's thought that less than 40 percent of people worldwide can actually properly digest lactose after childhood.

So, why do we put ourselves through the turmoil?

Because most of us tend to think that's "just the way it is" and don't really know anything different. But you may be amazed at how good you can feel when you do make some of these changes.

For me, I didn't have a whole lot of changes to make given that I rarely ate dairy anyway, except for the occasional bowl of ice cream or a slice or sprinkle of cheese on my dinners. But again, it all came down to me finding delicious replacements that I could have instead.

First, there are plenty of non-dairy milks on the market that are great for drinking, cooking, baking, etc.

- Almond milk
- Coconut milk
- Flaxseed milk
- Cashew milk
- Rice milk
- Hemp milk

There is also a great plant-based milk called Ripple that I love to use in my protein shakes every morning because of the smooth texture it gives them.

You can find sweetened, unsweetened, vanilla and chocolate varieties of these milks and simply use them in place of your dairy milk as you normally would. If you're feeling particularly industrious, you can also make many of these milks at home by soaking almonds (or other nuts) for several days and then straining them.

There are also non-dairy varieties of yogurt and ice cream made from these milks, many of which are quite good. One of my favorite desserts is vanilla no-sugar-added coconut milk ice cream with carob (or cocoa) powder or powdered peanut butter sprinkled on top. Yum!

Now, I will admit … finding a delicious dairy-free cheese has been more challenging for me. Most of them have a consistency and/or taste that I don't like. But there are lots of options out there and they're all subject to individual tastes.

Now that my adrenals are stronger and I am healthier overall, I have added cheese back in on an occasional basis. It is still very important for me to make sure I am consuming the *right* cheese though. So, I make sure to choose products that are organic and come from cows that were not treated with antibiotics or growth hormones. I also particularly like to get my cheese from local farmers at the farmer's market, where I can talk to them about their production process and ingredients.

LEARN MORE

Check out some of my favorite dairy-free items and recipes on my blog at *www.LiveaFastLife.com* or through my "De-Tox" course at *www.DeClutterDeToxDeStress.com.*

SUGAR

Sugar can be more addictive than cocaine.

Yes, you read that right.

Studies have shown that sugar stimulates the brain in the same way as hard drugs like cocaine. That's why it can be so difficult, almost impossible, for many people to stop consuming sugary products.

Believe me, I know.

I had a *major* sweet tooth for many, many years. Pretty much from the time I was little right up into my early 30s. I would eat cupcakes, cake, ice cream, brownies, cookies, you name it. And it wasn't until I went on the restricted diet for a whopping six months that I was able to finally break that addiction.

That's because when you're trying to go sugar-free, your body literally has to de-tox from it!

It's an old saying — "having a sweet tooth" — but those feelings you get after dinner, where you just *have* to have something sweet or you simply cannot resist having a piece of cake or pie when it's in front of you … those are addictive behaviors.

Yes, I'm sure you enjoy the taste. But more than likely, you're craving those sugary foods because you want the "high" that they give you. Whether you realize it consciously or not.

But the scary part isn't even that you might be addicted to sugar and not even know it. The scary part is what it is doing to your body.

Sugar consumption can lead to:

- Fatty liver disease
- Insulin resistance
- Obesity
- Cardiovascular disease
- Type II diabetes
- Heart disease
- Cancer

Basically, it wreaks havoc on your body's hormones and metabolic processes, which over time leads to serious disease.

Unfortunately, as a society, we focus mostly on the treatments or "cures" for these types of conditions, instead of trying to prevent them in the first place by changing our diet and what we consume.

By the time I went to the naturopathic doctor, I already was having issues with my liver. I was also having a lot of pre-diabetic symptoms, which blew my mind, as I had no family history, was fairly young and maintained a healthy weight.

But I did, however, consume massive amounts of sugar. And I hadn't ever made the connection between my sugar habit and my liver health.

I also had always had very shaky hands for as long as I can remember and was used to telling people, *"Oh, that's just the way I am …"* when they would ask about the shakiness.

Come to find out, when I finally took control of my diet and cut out the sugar altogether, my shakiness went away altogether as well.

Apparently, it was not just *how I was.*

Right before I began seeing the naturopathic doctor, I also had been experiencing what I thought were night sweats. It was unnerving to me because my overactive imagination started wondering if I was going through perimenopause; I thought I was too young to be having hot flashes.

However, when I explained the symptom to the naturopath — how I'd wake up out of a deep sleep feeling clammy and sweaty and then have to try to go back to sleep — he immediately identified it as my blood sugar. More specifically, that my blood sugar was dropping sharply in the middle of the night (from the constant roller coaster I was keeping it on with my sugar consumption), which was waking me up and causing the sweating.

I honestly wouldn't have believed it myself, except that these episodes went away entirely as soon as I changed my diet.

Put good things in = get good results out.

So, how does a self-admitted sugar junkie go sugar free? Well, it ain't easy. But it *can* be done.

First, you *have* to give your body time to de-tox and adjust. Remember, your body has quite literally become addicted to sugar, so it will take some time to "get clean." Hopefully, it won't take you six whole months like it did for me! But you do need to give yourself at least 30 days.

Then, just like with gluten and dairy, it's key to find healthier alternatives that you enjoy. There are alternative sweeteners that are better for you and still taste good, but you will most likely have to adjust to the taste. Nothing is going to taste *exactly* like sugar.

I want to take a moment here to point out that when I am talking about alternative sweeteners, I am NOT talking about those that come in little pink, blue or yellow packets. Those are chemically created, and often just as bad as, if not worse than, real sugar.

I am referring to healthier, *natural* options like:

- Stevia
- Xylitol *(Some people may experience a laxative effect from Xylitol, so be sure to try it in small amounts at first to test how your body responds. Xylitol is also toxic and fatal to dogs, so be sure to keep it secure and away from your pets!)*
- Honey *(Preferably from local beekeepers because the FDA allows honey sellers to label their ingredients as "honey" if the product contains no more than 50% high-fructose corn syrup. And local honey is also great for preventing environmental allergies in your particular region.)*
- Dates
- Molasses
- Pure maple syrup
- Coconut sugar (I like to use this in place of brown sugar!)

Generally speaking, I use stevia the most, with xylitol and coconut sugar tying for second. Although I don't particularly love the flavor of honey or dates on their own, I have used both as sweeteners in baking and they've been delicious.

Again, it did take a little while to adjust. But for me, I think the transition was made easier by being off of sugar completely for six months. Because then, when I added in products or recipes that used stevia, I really didn't have as dramatic of a reaction as someone who may have just had sugar two days ago.

Some people notice a bitter taste when it comes to stevia, although I never have. And what I particularly love about this sweetener is that it comes in both liquid and powder form.

So, if I am baking, I can measure out the powdered stevia as I would with regular sugar. But I also like to carry a small squeeze bottle of liquid stevia (usually in a yummy flavor) in my purse, so I can use it for my decaf, non-dairy coffee drinks from Starbucks!

You can find TONS of delicious recipes online for cookies, brownies, pies, cakes, muffins and donuts that use these alternative sweeteners. But you *will* most likely have to make a lot of your sweet treats at home — at least, until the market at large catches up.

❧❧ ──────➙ LEARN MORE ◅•────── ◂◂

Check out some of my favorite recipes that use alternative sweeteners on my Pinterest boards at *www.Pinterest.com/ LiveaFastLife.*

As of right now, you aren't going to find a lot of naturally sweetened items in the grocery store. You may find a couple here and there, especially if you shop at a health-centered store or one with a large organic and natural department. But for the most part, these products are still few and far between.

This is why it is so important to be prepared!

As I changed my diet, I learned to never assume that there will be something I can eat when I go to a friend's house or a party. So, I will often bring my own! Whether it's just a protein bar in my purse or my own dessert at a holiday dinner, I don't shy away from fending for myself and you shouldn't either!

The other thing you need to keep in mind when cutting sugar out of your diet is that sugar is NOT only in traditionally "sweet" foods. Sugar is in *everything*. And I do mean everything.

If you've never paid attention before, start checking the sugar content on the labels of all your products — beverages, snacks, pasta sauces, pickles, salad dressings … everything. You'd be surprised at how much sugar you're ingesting in other products throughout the day when you don't even realize it.

This was one of the biggest surprises for me. So now, I make sure that I check all my products in the grocery store, not just the obvious ones.

LEARN MORE

Check out some of my favorite sugar-free items and recipes on my blog at *www.LiveaFastLife.com* or through my "De-Tox" course at *www.DeClutterDeToxDeStress.com.*

GMOs

Another one of the big changes I made to my diet when I decided to "clean up" my body was to cut out GMOs.

For those of you who aren't sure exactly what GMOs (or genetically modified organisms) are, the Non-GMO Project's definition is *"a plant, animal, microorganism or other organism whose genetic makeup has been modified using recombinant DNA methods (also called gene splicing), gene modification or transgenic technology."* Sounds delicious, right?

So, how does this apply to the food you're eating?

Well, most packaged food products contain ingredients like corn and soy (even ones you wouldn't expect) and unfortunately, the majority of those crops in the United States are now genetically modified. And often, even the few crops that are *not* modified, end up being "contaminated" by wind drift from neighboring fields. This means that, every day, we are consuming foods that have been altered and "modified" by scientists.

Most of the developed nations in the world consider GMOs to be unsafe for human consumption and have, therefore, passed regulations to ban or limit their use. However, the United States government has approved them *"based on studies conducted by the same corporations that created them and profit from their sale"* (NonGMOProject.org) and only just recently (in 2016) passed a rather convoluted law about labelling them.

Although labeling is now required, the details are still sketchy at best — giving food producers several options other than simply printing the words on the package, including the use of a symbol (that has not been designed yet), an 800 number that consumers have to call to get GMO information on a product or a QR code that has to be scanned by a smartphone for information. Obviously, the latter options are more difficult and less likely to be followed up on by consumers while standing in the middle of a grocery store aisle and outright impossible for some, who may not have access to the proper technology.

This is why it is so important not to just assume that something is safe for you to eat just because you find it on the supermarket shelves. You have to remember that the food industry is a *business.* It is predominantly run by some major players who look out for their wallet, not your well-being. So, it is up to YOU to watch out for your own health.

Although it is a bit difficult to avoid GMOs because of the lack of clear labelling laws, I did begin purchasing NON-GMO products whenever possible and continue to do so. You can find more information on the non-GMO Project, a non-profit organization that provides education, as well as non-GMO product verification, at *www.NonGMOProject.org.*

But more importantly (because I am still not a GMO expert *and don't claim to be!*), I would recommend that everyone try to stick to whole foods and avoid packaged and processed foods altogether, as much as possible. After all, it's about getting back to basics and the way food was made to be — natural!

❯❯ ─────────→ *F.A.S.T.* TIP ←───────── ◗◗

Shop the perimeter of the grocery store. That's where the fresh foods are located. Skip the aisles that are in the middle of the store.

ORGANICS

I'll be the first to admit: I never really paid much attention to organics before my health crisis. I'm sure they existed … it's not like they're a recent discovery from the past couple years. But I think it's easy for most people to just sort of sail right past them, if you're not particularly looking for them — especially because the price tag on organic items can be twice that (or more!) of the non-organic items.

But as I began to pay more attention to what I put in my body, it only made sense that I would start choosing organic fruits and vegetables.

Organic food is grown without pesticides, GMOs, synthetic fertilizers or radiation. At first glance, you probably would want all your food to be made in this way, right? But unfortunately, that's not always the case.

This is why, again, it is SO important to pay attention to what you're buying and consuming.

Unlike GMOs, there is a labeling system for organic foods. But it is still important to know what the different labels mean. Unfortunately, it's not black and white.

100% Organic – product is made with 100% organic ingredients

Organic – product is made with at least 95% organic ingredients

Made with Organic Ingredients – product is made with a minimum of 70% organic ingredients (and includes no GMOs)

Products with less than 70% organic ingredients may list those organic ingredients on the side of the package, but make no "organic" claims on the front of the package.

Source: From organic.org

Now, I try to buy organic all the time if I can. If I go to a grocery store that doesn't carry something organic, I will still buy a non-organic item once in a while, but I try not to make it a habit. There are also some foods that are *okay* to buy non-organic if necessary — basically, ones that have a thick outer skin or layer that you don't consume, like avocados, bananas, onions, kiwis and melons.

When buying other produce, like tomatoes, berries, lettuces, cucumbers, peppers, apples, pears and grapes, it is extremely important to buy organic so you're not subjecting your body to the pesticide residue left on the exposed skin of the food.

MEATS

I have thought about becoming a vegetarian a LOT.

Not only for the health benefits, but mostly because I am *extremely* sensitive when it comes to animals and I don't like to think about the fact that I am eating them. (Like, to the point that I have to hold my hand in front of my face and avert my eyes when I pass one of those chicken trucks on the road.)

For a long time, I put off becoming a vegetarian because I was overwhelmed by the thought of it. I didn't know what I would possibly eat all the time, so I just never really gave it a go. Then, when I became gluten-free, I felt even more intimidated by the idea because that cut out a lot of the pasta dishes that I figured would be a "go to" as a vegetarian.

But, I finally gave in and decided to give it a try back in 2013 — basically, right before my health took a nosedive. I had successfully been eating meatless for about a month or so, when I finally began seeing my "dream team" for my adrenal issues.

While discussing my diet one day with my NMT, she suggested that I may need meat in my diet in order to consume enough protein to heal my adrenals. Although I didn't immediately go back to consuming meat after our conversation, I did do some more research and discussed it with my naturopath, and ended up coming to the conclusion that it wasn't the best time for me to be a vegetarian because I needed even *more* protein than usual in my weakened condition.

So, I went back to meat and still eat it (for now), although I am a lot choosier about it these days.

For one, I don't eat pork at all. This is not to say that there's anything necessarily bad about pork. I just have never been a huge fan (except for bacon), so it really wasn't even an issue for me. Same with seafood — I never really ate it that much before. So, the biggest change I made was to actually *add in* more fish. My naturopath advised me to stick to the "big guys" in the sea, like salmon and swordfish, and avoid the bottom feeders like shrimp, scallops and smaller fish, because they can contain more heavy metals.

I also began eating only antibiotic-free and hormone-free chicken and beef, as well as beef that was grass-fed and grass-finished (I learned this was an important distinction to make because cattle can sometimes be grass-fed but then "finished" with grain right before they go to slaughter. Clarifying that it was both grass-fed and grass-finished will ensure they had a no-grain diet.)

Again, this is where I suggest you watch "Food, Inc." for the whole story on this subject. But in a nutshell, the food industry often pumps chickens and cows full of antibiotics (to keep them from getting sick) and hormones (to get them bigger and meatier). Then, when we consume them, the same chemicals get passed into our bloodstream.

Not only can this mess with our hormone balance and cause our children to develop faster (i.e., developing breasts and pubic hair at a very young age), but it can also cause us to develop an antibiotic resistance. And this is just on our end. Don't even get me started on the poor chickens who are pumped up so big that they often literally cannot stand back up if they fall over in the overcrowded coops they are raised in (seriously, watch the movie).

Then, there is also the issue of how humanely the animals were raised and slaughtered. And this doesn't just pertain to how you feel emotionally about consuming them. It actually affects *your* health too.

Simply put, if a cow or chicken experiences a high level of stress right before it is slaughtered, its body will react in the same way that ours would — by going into "fight or flight" and releasing a bunch of chemicals, including adrenaline and cortisol.

However, when this happens right before slaughter and then their meat is passed along to us to eat, we end up consuming those chemicals as well. This can then affect our own bodily processes and reproductive systems.

Because of these chemicals, meat from animals that experience high levels of stress is often also tougher and even tasteless, as compared to the meat of animals that were humanely raised and slaughtered.

It's also important to be aware of the food *they* ate. If a cow that we eat consumed grain on a daily basis, that will be passed along to us as well. That's why those of us who eat a gluten-free or grain-free diet need to consume only grass-fed, grass-finished meats.

Bet you never really thought much about that, huh? I know I didn't.

I know it can sound like a lot on paper. But in actuality, it's a lot easier than you think. It's just about making a few changes and most importantly, *paying attention* to what you're putting in your body.

For me, it was also about being as "cleaned up" and "stripped down" as possible. I was already getting rid of the excess stuff around my house and shedding my toxic emotional baggage (more on that later), so it only made sense to get rid of the stuff that was physically toxic to my body as well.

I only have one body and it was a gift to me from God. So it is up to ME to take care of it and make sure I give it the best possible chance to function well for me. I may not be able to control everything in my environment all of the time. But I was ready to take control of the things I *could* change.

And believe me, my body thanked me for it. And yours will too.

Chapter 8

CLEANING UP MY BODY (ON THE OUTSIDE)

When I first went gluten-free, I did a major overhaul of all my cabinets. My *kitchen* cabinets.

I didn't even *think* about gluten lurking in my bathroom cabinets! But as I was about to find out, it was indeed.

One day, I was sitting in my apartment talking to my friend Lisa, who is sort of my health "guru," as she had already made a lot of the same lifestyle changes a few years prior. We were talking about beauty and skin care products when she asked me if I had checked the ingredients on mine.

Now, I'm sure if I had stopped to give it any amount of thought at all (which I really hadn't up to that point), I probably would've already known that I needed to replace many of my products if I wanted to be non-toxic. But in this moment, we were just talking about gluten. And up until then, I hadn't even considered the possibility that I may be taking in gluten through avenues other than my food.

Plus, I was using a skin care line at the time that is marketed as very "natural" and "earthy," so I thought for sure she was just overreacting. I figured I would go into the bathroom, pull out my moisturizer, read her the ingredients and smile as I put it back safely into my medicine cabinet.

Except that's not what happened.

I pulled out my supposedly-healthy moisturizer, looked at the ingredients list and there, plain as day, was "*wheat gluten*." Here, I had been working my butt off to overhaul my whole diet and learn to eat gluten-free, and I had been unknowingly slathering gluten all over my skin the whole time. Fabulous.

Now, if you're wondering why this matters, it's because *what goes on your body, goes in your body.*

Your skin is the largest organ in your body. And whatever you put on your skin, goes through your skin and into your bloodstream. That's how things like birth control patches and smoking cessation patches work — you put them on your skin and, within minutes, the medication starts entering your body.

So, it's no different when it comes to the products that we use on our bodies — things like lotion, deodorant, shower gel, soap, hairspray, sunscreen and cosmetics. Even the shampoo and conditioner that we use on our hair can seep through the skin on our scalp. Whatever ingredients are inside of them will soon be inside of us.

It's kind of a no-brainer. But, again, something you probably never really thought about (I know I didn't), until something gives you a *reason* to think about it.

After that discovery about the hidden dangers of my moisturizer, I started paying more attention to the ingredients that were in my other products and started educating myself on the effects they can have on your body.

And I did *not* like what I found.

Once again, here was all this information right there for me to read and learn if I just looked for it. Yet, the companies and manufacturers (in whom I had put my blind trust), didn't find it necessary to inform me. Because then I wouldn't want to buy their products.

Just like with the food, here I am reading about chemicals and other ingredients that are *known* carcinogens being put into the products that you and I use every single day. And are we being told this?

No.

Like most other Americans, I was just going along through life, *assuming* that if I bought something off the shelf in the store, it must not be harmful for me. Right?

Wrong.

In reality, the United States has not passed a federal law to regulate the safety of the ingredients used in personal care products since 1938.*

Yes, you read that right. As in, more than 75 years ago. And to make matters worse, the U.S. government has only banned 30 chemicals in personal care products. To give you a comparison, the European Union has banned more than 1,300 and restricted the use of more than 250 others.*

From Beautycounter.com

Pathetically sad, isn't it?

In fact, the U.S. Food and Drug Administration (FDA) states right on their website that *"Neither the law nor FDA regulations require specific tests to demonstrate the safety of individual products or ingredients. The law also does not require cosmetic companies to share their safety information with FDA."*

No, the reality is, it's up to the manufacturers themselves. *"Companies and individuals who manufacture or market cosmetics have a legal responsibility to ensure the safety of their products."*

So, if you're not getting the message yet … ***you can't assume that products are okay for you just because they're for sale in the United States.***

I wish that was the case, but unfortunately it's not. This is why it's up to us to educate ourselves and make the necessary changes. Because no one is going to do it for us.

When I decided to overhaul my products, it was a daunting task. (Much like when I overhauled the food in my kitchen.) It seemed like every item I picked up had one, 10 or 20 toxic chemicals in it! And it made me a little nauseated to know I had been blindly using them for years.

(And again … no wonder why we all know someone who has cancer.)

But what I tried to do (and what I recommend you do) is to take it one step at a time. Don't try to replace every single item all at once. Yes, you want to get them out of your life as soon as possible, but the reality is healthier products are also a lot more expensive than traditional ones, so you may not be able to replace everything at the same time.

What I did with a lot of products was wait until they ran out and then replaced them with a new, non-toxic alternative. If it was a product that would typically last a long time, like cosmetics or sunscreen, then I went ahead and replaced them right away. But for things like shampoo, conditioner, lotion and deodorant, I just finished off what I had and then replaced it with a healthier version.

So, what exactly is a healthier or non-toxic version?

Well, first I am going to tell you what it's *not*.

Products that say any of these words on the front of the package: "*natural*," "*pure*," "*simple*," "*minerals*," "*vitamins*" or have images of trees and plants and green and brown color schemes are **NOT** automatically non-toxic products.

They are products that have been specifically designed by a well-paid marketing team to *look* natural and organic.

Don't ever pick a product solely based on how it looks. The truth lies on the ingredients label.

So, what ingredients do you need to look for? Well, like I mentioned earlier, there are literally thousands. So it's not something you're going to be able to memorize for the store.

To make things a little easier when you're out shopping, I like to use the "Skin Deep" Database by the Environmental Working Group (EWG). You can find it on their website (*http://www.ewg.org/skindeep*) or download an app where you simply type in the name of a product and it will bring up a ranking showing you how toxic its ingredients are.

I try to only stick to products that are below a "5" in the EWG database, and if for some reason a product does not show up on the database and I'm unsure, I skip it altogether. I'd rather be safe than sorry.

common ingredients that you can start to look for as things to avoid:

- 1,4 - Dioxane
- Benzophenone
- BHA/BHT
- Carbon Black
- Coal Tar
- Cyanide
- Formaldehyde
- Homosalate
- Hydroquinone
- MEA/DEA/TEA
- Methylisothiazolinone (MIT)
- Parabens
- Paraphenylenediamine (PPD)
- Phenoxyethanol
- Phthalates
- Polyethylene Glycol (PEG)
- Sulfates (SLS and SLES)
- Synthetic or artificial flavors and fragrances
- Toluene
- Triclosan

This is only a small fraction of the harmful ingredients you will find in cosmetics and personal care products, but it will give you a great head start.

And if you're wondering why you should care …

These ingredients are known to cause a whole host of issues in the body, including (but not limited to):

- Endocrine disruption (hormonal issues)
- Kidney damage
- Cancerous tumors
- Birth defects
- Reproductive issues
- Heart disease
- Heart failure
- Neurologic impairment (brain damage)

We're not talking about a simple rash here. We're talking about serious, life-altering (or potentially life-threatening) consequences.

I know it's infuriating (and if you're not infuriated yet, you should be), but I share this with you not to discourage or scare you, but to ***motivate*** you and ***educate*** you.

I was unaware of all of this myself, just a few short years ago. But having gone through my own health crisis and having watched both of my parents pass away from invasive cancers, I decided to take control of the things that I *can* change (and pray about the things I can't!).

The upside is that there *are* truly healthier options available on the market. So again, check your labels and, when in doubt, call the company and ask them directly.

LEARN MORE

Check out some of my favorite non-toxic products on my blog at *www.LiveaFastLife.com* or through my "De-Tox" course at *www.DeClutterDeToxDeStress.com.*

Homemade products are also a great option and really the best way to know 100% what you are using. You can easily make soap, shampoo, toothpaste, conditioner and even deodorant at home using just a few simple ingredients like baking soda, apple cider vinegar, lemon juice and essential oils. You can check my blog and e-course for suggestions on this as well.

The point is to *do something*.

Please don't just cover your ears, close your eyes and sing "*la la la*" because it's not going to make it go away. It's up to YOU to take care of yourself and your family.

After I had cleared out my home of all the clutter and cleaned up what I put in and on my body, I knew that I had to go a step further and make changes to the products I used around my home as well.

After all, the ingredients in those products would eventually make their way into my body as well, by being breathed in through my lungs, absorbed through my skin or even taken in through my eyes or mouth.

Think about it … your dish detergent touches all the surfaces you eat off of, and your laundry detergent and fabric softener touch the clothes you wear and the sheets you sleep on. Your kitchen counters and bathroom surfaces get cleaned with chemicals, the carpets your children and pets play on are sprinkled with powders, and even the chemicals you spray into the air as an air freshener or release through a candle will be breathed in through your nose and mouth.

It's surprising and almost ludicrous that most of us don't really think about all of these products before we use them. But it all comes back to that *assumption* that we don't have to.

But the truth unfortunately is, as I researched my household products, I just found more of the same. I kept finding known carcinogens and other health-damaging ingredients in practically everything I (and the rest of America) used on a daily basis.

Ingredients that cause:

- Organ toxicity
- Eye and skin irritation
- Neurological damage
- Endocrine disruption (hormonal issues)
- Impaired breathing/asthma
- Reproductive system damage
- Liver and kidney damage
- Low birth weight
- Respiratory disorders
- Cancer

All this was hidden under the pleasant disguise of a "flowery meadow" or the supposed "healthy benefit" of germ killing. In actuality, many of these products are doing much more harm than good.

I know it might be twisting to your brain to think that you actually don't need to douse yourself in hand sanitizer or cover your kitchen in bleach to be healthy. But it's true. Contrary beliefs result from a lot of marketing gurus working their magic on you.

And they've done an amazingly good job, haven't they?

Anti-bacterial and anti-microbial products actually contain the harmful ingredient, Triclosan, which has been shown in studies to cause endocrine disruption (particularly to the thyroid), skin irritation and, ironically, anti-biotic resistance.

On the other hand, I stopped using antibacterial products five years ago (when I changed my products and diet), and have only been sick one time in those five years (as compared to before when I tended to be sick 3-4 times every year with sinus infections, bronchitis, the flu, strep throat and stomach bugs). In my case at least, this just goes to show how unnecessary they are.

It's about retraining your brain.

The truth is, you can actually do most of your cleaning with those magic ingredients I mentioned earlier: baking soda, apple cider vinegar and lemon juice.

But if you feel better buying packaged products that come from the store, there are still healthier, non-toxic versions available. You just need to be sure again not to fall for the marketing schemes on the package, and to check the actual ingredient lists for things you *don't* want like:

- 1,4 - Dioxane
- 2-Butoxyethanol
- Ammonia
- Chlorine
- Perchloroethylene (PERC)

- Phthalates
- Quarternary Ammonium Compounds (Quats)
- Sodium Hydroxide
- Triclosan
- Toluene
- Chlorofoam & Carbon Tetrachloride
- Galaxolide
- Ethanolamine
- NPEs
- Phosphates
- Silica Powder
- Sodium Dichloroisocyanurate Dihydrate
- Sulfates
- Trisodium Nitrilotriacetate
- Methylene Chloride

Sounds like a chem lab, doesn't it?

And that's kind of the point.

When God led me to make all of these changes in my life, it was about stripping down, getting rid of all the excess and toxins, and living a "cleaned up," back-to-basics kind of life. So, it only made sense that I would get rid of all these man-made, extremely *un*natural things that I had been putting on and in my body.

No, I haven't gone totally caveman and started cooking over an open fire and washing in the river. But, I *have* stripped away a LOT of stuff that I didn't need in my life, as well as things that were bringing me down and causing me harm or stress.

That's what a "*F.A.S.T.*" life is all about.

It's about living life full of joy, peace and abundance without all the unnecessary baggage. It's about having a healthy body, a healthy spirit and a healthy home.

And the more God led me through this process, the more clear and obvious it all became to me.

Of course I don't need all these gadgets, books, movies, knick-knacks and whatever else to be happy ... God didn't create all that. We did.

Of course my body doesn't perform well or stay healthy when I fill it with foods and beverages that are made of chemicals and artificial ingredients. God didn't create all that. We did.

And *of course* our bodies were never meant to function under the constant application of toxin-laden products and cleaners. God didn't create all of that. We did.

It was all starting to come together. My home was cleaned up, my body was cleaned up and there really was only one thing left to do.

It was time to clean up my spirit.

Chapter 9

BYE-BYE, EMOTIONAL BAGGAGE

When my body first began to feel like it was falling apart,
I wasn't totally surprised.

I mean, I *had* already been through an extremely stressful relationship
and the death of my father, and was maintaining a pretty bad diet and
sleep schedule when the symptoms started to show up. So, it didn't take
a brain surgeon to find a link.

But what *did* surprise me was the timing of it all.

Here I had been living at the extreme height of adrenaline pretty much
all day, every day when I was with my ex. Yet, I was totally fine the whole
time I was with him. Sure, I had the normal cold and flu that I got every
year. But other than some heart palpitations once in a while when things
were getting really heated, my body had held up pretty well.

Or so I thought.

But that's the thing about your health — it's not just about the *physical*.
In fact, the physical is usually just the end result of what's going on in
your body emotionally.

Emotions have an effect on our bodies, plain and simple. And most people acknowledge that to some degree. They know how anxiety over public speaking can cause a stomach ache or too much crying can cause a headache. It's also pretty widely accepted that stress has a negative impact on your health and can cause high blood pressure or heart attacks.

But what most of us (again, me included, up until a few years ago) fail to acknowledge is the day-to-day, constant connection between our emotions and our physical health.

Meaning, you cannot have extreme emotional experiences (particularly negative ones) and expect them *not* to have an effect on you physically. Whether it's a one-time event or something that goes on for a prolonged period, emotional traumas *will* manifest in your bodies as physical symptoms one way or another.

This is especially true if you don't address the emotions properly and instead avoid them or stuff them down inside, like many of us do.

This is exactly why my body didn't fall apart until *after* I had ended the abusive relationship.

During the time of actual stress, my body was in survival mode. It was doing everything it could to keep me going, keep me functioning and keep me safe. It wasn't until that "threat" had finally been minimized and my body could switch out of survival mode that the damage started showing.

I was consciously in survival mode during that time too. There were brief moments here and there where I really thought about what was going on … but for the most part, I would glaze over it and just focus on getting through that day as peacefully as possible.

Even the death of my father unfortunately got sort of glazed over, because it happened at the exact same time that I was trying to separate myself from my ex. With so many overwhelming emotions happening at once, my mind sort of checked out of them altogether and I sort of floated through the days, just going through the motions.

It's what we do as human beings when our bodies and minds are pushed to the limit — it's a natural survival mechanism. And the good thing is, it works. It gets you through that moment, that day, that crisis.

But the bad news is that if you never go back and actually deal with those emotions at some point, they *will* come back to haunt you later.

You may think you're doing just fine. You got through it, you survived, you're moving on. Except now, you've gained 50 lbs. Or you suddenly can't sleep through the night without Ambien. Or you've developed migraines that you never had before.

Just because those emotions aren't showing on the surface doesn't mean they're not still there, deep inside.

And when I started cleaning up my life and really paying attention to my body after my adrenal fatigue diagnosis, I found a *LOT* of baggage hiding inside.

There was the obvious: the abusive relationship, the death of my father, the death of my mother, the end of several friendships and the feelings I had stuffed from the toxic work environment I had been in.

But once I opened the floodgates, the waters just kept coming.

Old beliefs and feelings came up about my family, my childhood, my adolescence, my self-esteem, trust, money, fear and value. The things

I hadn't even realized I had "stuffed" until they desperately gasped for recognition were suddenly fighting their way to the surface.

It was why my body had been "programmed" for anxiety, nervousness and fear since I was a child. It was why I was a shoe-in for adrenal fatigue and why I had so many of the habits that I did.

It started to become really clear why I seemed to always feel so tired, so worn-down and stressed-out just under the surface. Even on good days. Because my body had been holding on with white knuckles for so many years and I hadn't even realized it.

And all that these trapped emotions really wanted from me was recognition. I needed to acknowledge them, to really let myself sit in them and feel them. So, I could then finally and truly *let them go*.

It was a scary revelation, to say the least. No one likes to address the "yucky" stuff. That's why it's so much easier to just avoid it and zone out in a Netflix marathon instead.

But a few months or years and many Netflix marathons later, you find yourself feeling sick and tired all the time, with little reserves for the daily stresses of life. And you start to wonder why you can't just feel lighter and more joyful.

Well, the answer is pretty simple …

You can't fly with lead weights strapped to your heels.

You have to take a deep breath, put your big girl (or boy) pants on and dive into those issues head first.

So that's exactly what I did.

The first time I really realized that there might be some trapped emotions inside that I needed to deal with was that night I broke down after de-cluttering my sentimental items.

When the lump in my chest finally made its way up to the surface and I had a nice long cry, I thought, "Okay, *maybe* there is some unresolved grief that I wasn't aware of."

But I still didn't really do much to address it at that time. I did talk to my roommate that night, which helped. And I figured that's just how grief goes — it comes in waves, sometimes seemingly out of the blue, and then it dissipates again until the next surge.

However, the more I delved into healing my adrenals, the more I realized that I had to go back and work out a lot of unresolved emotions to get my body to calm down. It wasn't just the abusive relationship that had gotten my body to stay in a virtually permanent state of fight-or-flight. Many other events prior had also contributed to it.

So, it was high time for me to actually acknowledge the emotions and let myself really do the work, so I could be free of them for good.

I didn't really know how to go about doing that though.

Enter my dream team.

Emotions tend to "live" in different parts of the body. For instance, anxiety and stress live in the stomach (which leads to "butterflies" or stomach aches when you're nervous) and grief lives in the chest (which is why people often feel "heartache" over a loss).

So, when I would go to see my naturopath, she would recommend certain vitamins and minerals to help support those particular organs or areas of my body that were under duress. It wasn't so much a direct-fix, as much as an added help. I still had to do the emotional work, but the supplements helped my body to keep trucking physically during the process.

I also continued to see the neuromuscular therapist, who worked to "retrain" those over-activated reflexes in my body and get them to return to their natural states.

But the most important thing that I did was simply to address the old baggage.

Seems almost too simple to be true, right? But that's the beauty of it. I didn't have to go to a million doctors or try a dozen different medications to feel better. All I had to do was be willing to dive inside and bring whatever was hiding in there out into the light.

Easier said than done though, right?

Agreed. I'm not going to lie … it wasn't a fun process for me and if you do the same, it won't be for you either. But what I can promise you is, ***IT'S WORTH IT.***

And it's really the only way that you will ever be able to finally feel free of all that old baggage you've been dragging around (knowingly or unknowingly) for years.

So, how do you do it?

Well, I don't know exactly what will work for you, but I do want to share what worked for me. That's what this book and my blog are all about — sharing my experiences, so hopefully you can be encouraged and inspired in your own lives.

So for me, my emotional healing came from a combination of affirmations, meditation and prayer. Now, I know each one of those can be an intimidating concept all on its own, so let me break it down for you.

AFFIRMATIONS

I had always had a pretty negative attitude about affirmations (kind of ironic, huh?). I had, of course, heard about them over the years and had even practiced them a little, back when I did the social anxiety program in my 20s.

But overall, I always thought they wouldn't really work for me because, basically, I would call BS on myself.

No matter how many times I recited, "*I'm a super person and gosh darnit, people like me!,*" I would immediately think "***NOT.***"

Ok, I'm being sarcastic here … those are not the kind of affirmations I did.

The point is, I had a pretty negative outlook overall (I'm sorry to say), so I just didn't think I would ever believe myself, no matter how many flowery statements I recited.

But what I hadn't realized up to that point was that I was looking at affirmations all wrong.

It didn't really matter if I believed them or not. At least not at first anyway. It was just about re-training my brain and the "programming" it had been running for so long.

See, when we think the same thoughts repeatedly over and over, we form programs in our brain. After enough reinforcement, it becomes almost automatic. And soon, it becomes so ground-in, that it becomes a belief, whether the original thought was even true or not.

For example, let's say you were around during the time of Christopher Columbus. Growing up, you were taught the world was flat. Your schoolbook said it was flat. Your teacher said it was flat. You'd stand at the edge of the ocean and look out into the horizon and see the drop-off at the end. World = flat.

Then one day, this Columbus guy comes along and says the world is round. Now even if you believe him, your brain is going to have a heck of a time wrapping itself around that new thought, because you've been thinking the opposite for so long.

It becomes an automatic thought. World = flat. World = flat. You would have to now consciously remind yourself … *"Oh yeah, world = round."*

Well the same goes for how we think about ourselves.

Most of us have been forming the beliefs that we have about ourselves and the world since we were little children. We start forming thoughts and opinions based on our childhoods and how we grew up, and then, over time, those thoughts get reaffirmed until they become beliefs.

The problem is, those thoughts may never have even been true in the first place.

Here's another example. Let's say as a child, your father walks out on you and your family. You think it must be because you weren't good enough. After all, if you were good enough, lovable enough, perfect enough … he would've stayed.

So you go through life, thinking these same thoughts over and over. When a friendship fades, it's because you weren't good enough. When a relationship doesn't work out, it's because you're not lovable enough. When a job doesn't come through, you weren't perfect enough.

The problem is you, you, you.

Except what if that isn't the truth?

What if the friendship ended because you grew into two different people and no longer felt the bond you once had? And the relationship ended because the other person had their own issues they hadn't dealt with? And the job didn't work out because you're actually *over*-qualified?

And most importantly ... what if you realized that your father didn't leave you all those years ago because you weren't lovable? In fact, it had nothing to do with you at all. What if you realized your father left because of his own issues with commitment and responsibility, or because he and your mother were incapable of forming a partnership that was mutually supportive and healthy?

And for all that time ... you've been basing the beliefs you have about yourself and the world on nothing but a lie, a misconception, an incorrect perspective.

That would really shake things up, huh?

Well, I'm going to venture a guess and say you are probably believing some untruths about yourself this very moment.

They may not be as intense as the examples I offered here, but I'm sure you have some negative thought patterns to some degree, because we all do. It's just a fact of life.

But the good news is, we *can* retrain our brains.

And that's where the affirmations come in. It's not about trying to "fool" yourself into believing something. It's about stopping the old tapes from playing and starting new ones in their place.

It's about getting out of those old ruts in your brain and starting new thought patterns that actually make you feel good, happy and strong.

What you will actually say is up to you and, of course, depends on your own personal situation. Affirmations that worked for me may not work for you because we all have different issues. But more than likely, you're probably already pretty aware of what your beliefs are, so now it's just about taking the time to flip them around into something positive.

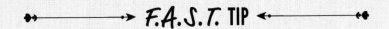

F.A.S.T. TIP

There's no right or wrong way to establish new, more positive thought patterns and no magic amount of time or number of repetitions, but here are a few tips:

- Repeat them at least once or twice a day, every day.

- Do it at the same time every day (when you first get up or when you climb into bed at night are usually good times).

- Say them aloud or write them down as opposed to just saying them in your head.

- Record yourself reciting them on a voice memo on your phone and then listen to them as you fall asleep.

- Write them down on Post-It notes and stick them where you'll see them every day (like your bedroom mirror or the console of your car).

You may not believe what you're saying at first and that's okay. It took a long time for you to dig that rut, so it's not going to just magically go away overnight. But the more you practice the new thoughts, the easier it will get.

If you think …	Try thinking this instead …
I'm too ugly/fat/skinny/etc.	• *I am beautiful just the way I am.* • *I am uniquely me.* • *I love my body and am grateful for my health.*
I'm not good enough.	• *I am good enough just the way I am.* • *I already have everything I need.* • *I am a valuable woman (or man) of worth.*
Nothing ever works out for me.	• *There are new opportunities around every corner.* • *I am grateful God protects me from going down the wrong paths.*

Again, these are just a few examples. You can sit down and write out ones that work for you. The important thing is to start combatting those negative thoughts ***ASAP***.

It may feel strange at first (in fact, it most likely will), but push through the awkwardness and keep going. Don't worry about what others think, and practice your affirmations in a time and space where you'll feel comfortable, so you won't feel embarrassed or worried about being interrupted.

Remember, God does not want us walking around constantly berating ourselves and knocking ourselves down. So don't feel guilty or ashamed about feeling good about yourself!

It's time to speak truth over yourself and tell those lies in your head to get lost. They've been shacking up in there for too long and it's about time you served them with an eviction notice.

MEDITATION

Meditation is another one of those terms that had always seemed pretty elusive to me. Of course, I had heard a lot over the years about how beneficial it is to your health and I had even tried a couple of times to give it a whirl, only to end up frustrated because I could never succeed in getting my mind to "quiet down."

But it wasn't until I approached meditation in a new way that it started to actually work for me.

First, let me clarify … when I talk about meditation, I am not talking about sitting with my legs crossed and saying "ohm."

What I am talking about is the actual definition of meditation — *to think deeply or focus one's mind for a period of time for religious or spiritual purposes or as a method of relaxation* (Wikipedia).

Simply put, it's about being quiet and being *still*.

After ending up with stage-four adrenal fatigue, I realized that I hardly ever let myself be still. Like totally, completely still — physically *and* mentally.

It's just not how our world operates. Everyone around us is always go, go, go ... so it's easy to get caught up in the mix.

But even if I *did* slow down long enough to rest physically, my mind NEVER stopped. I've always been a bit of an over-analyzer, so my brain was always going, going, going.

That's why I struggled for so long with not being able to fall asleep at night (as do many other people), because the first chance I gave my brain to unwind was when my head hit the pillow. It would gleefully jump for joy at the opportunity and proceed to unleash all the thoughts from that day, the day before and the day to come, all while I fitfully tried to get some rest.

This is why it was so important for me to learn to *intentionally* rest at some point during the day, so my mind could get a break. And I'm guessing, it probably is for you too.

And really, that's all meditation is — the *intentional* focusing and relaxing of your mind.

I finally gave up the notion that I was supposed to have a completely blank mind, devoid of all thoughts and realized that it was more about slowing down and relaxing. Thoughts can still come and go, but I don't have to give them weight and pay attention to them. I can simply let them float on through and stay relaxed.

So again, you're probably thinking, how do you do this?

Well, for me, I found the most effective way for me to meditate is actually to do something I refer to as "active meditation." I have no idea if that is a real term or not. But if it's not, I am officially coining it here.

What I mean by that is, instead of trying to wipe my brain of all thoughts and sit in nothingness, I intentionally focus on a particular scene. The scene itself varies — sometimes it's a beach, sometimes a field of wildflowers, sometimes a brook and a waterfall — but every time, I have a purpose and a reason for being there.

Now before I get into the purpose, let me clarify what I mean by "being" there. No, I do not think I am really going to a beach or a waterfall. And no, I am not talking about being magically transported to another place. In fact, if you *are* able to do that, I don't even want to know about it.

I am talking about "going there" in your mind. In the same way you can daydream or visualize about anything else, except this involves a little more concentrated effort.

Think about this: if you visualize yourself being on a roller coaster in full detail — getting into the seat and buckling up, the nerves of waiting for the car to start moving, the slow ascent up the first hill and the stomach-dropping look down right before you drop — your body will probably start to react like it's real, right? Heart racing, breathing fast, tightened stomach … the whole deal.

That's because our subconscious minds don't know the difference between when we're really experiencing something and when we're just thinking about it. So, the key is to use that to your advantage for relaxing and emotional health. Instead of visualizing yourself on a roller coaster, you visualize being somewhere relaxing, somewhere safe and serene.

And this is where the purpose I mentioned before comes into play.

Instead of just lollygagging around on the beach or hanging out in the field of flowers, I usually have a purpose for going there and that is to release whatever emotions or baggage that have been weighing on me.

Example: Maybe I am worried about a friend's child who is sick, I got irritated with a coworker at the office and I am stressed about bills. If I am meditating about being at the beach, then I will visualize walking along the sand and picking up shells. Each time I pick up a shell, I will "put" one of those issues (and all of the thoughts and feelings attached to it) into that shell and toss it into the ocean — symbolizing me letting it go and giving it back to God. Or maybe I'm "washing" them off of me in the waterfall or tossing them into the creek with the flowers.

The point is, I visualize releasing these thoughts and emotions, so I can *feel* more relaxed and light in reality.

Sound weird?

It's okay if it does. I had some doubts too when my OT first taught me this technique. But almost instantly, I was able to feel the difference in my body — my anxiety was lessened, my mind felt more clear and my stomach (which was usually clenched 24/7) felt more relaxed.

And the more often I practiced it, the better I felt. In fact, still to this day, I can usually tell when it's been too long since I've "released" stuff because I will literally start to feel weighed down and I know it's time to go lighten my load.

Even if you don't want to try an active meditation like this, you can do something simpler like a deep breathing exercise or a progressive muscle relaxation where you just focus on your breathing or tensing and then relaxing each muscle in your body.

The goal is simply to quiet your mind, relax your body and let go of anything you've been holding on to.

PRAYER

I am going to start this section out by saying that I acknowledge that prayer is a very personal thing, so I am in no way going to tell you how you should do it.

I am simply going to share with you what worked for me and encourage you to try prayer if you haven't before.

Having grown up as a Catholic, prayer to me meant reciting a bunch of words that I memorized as a child. It was a lot of flowery talk that I didn't really understand or even stop to consider. It was just programmed in my brain and came out automatically during the occasional visit to mass.

But it wasn't until God got a hold of me as an adult that I started having a personal relationship with Him and began praying to Him like I was talking to a friend or my Father.

And it wasn't until I started doing *that*, that I realized I would never be totally healed without it.

Now, prayer is an essential part of my day (usually the beginning to my day). It's when I spend some personal time with God, let Him know what I am struggling with, ask for help with certain things and maybe ask for His direction on others.

Again, it's a very personal thing and one that will be different for every single person. But the most important part to remember is that you are *not* on your own.

You don't have to drag yourself through your life day to day, just barely hanging on, trying to bear all the weight on your own two shoulders.

You can lay your burdens down daily at His feet and ask Him to help you.

"Come to me, all who labor and are heavy laden, and I will give you rest. ²⁹ Take my yoke upon you, and learn from me, for I am gentle and lowly in heart, and you will find rest for your souls. ³⁰ For my yoke is easy, and my burden is light."
– Matthew 11:28-30 (ESV) –

Life won't necessarily get easier — you will still have trials and storms to go through — but with God's help, you will be more able to withstand them and still find joy in the midst of them.

It's the reason I was not only able to go on from both my parents' passings, but to actually become even *more* grateful and *more* joyful than I was before.

Prayer is a concept that is too big, too awesome and too mind-blowing for me to put into words here. So, instead I will simply encourage you to go to Him on your own and invite Him into your heart and your life.

Stop trying to do it all on your own.

Let Him help you and let Him make your burden light.

It's time for you to start living the fabulous, abundant life that you were meant to live.

Chapter 10

BUCKET-LIST LIVING

Years ago, I wrote a "life to-do list" because I knew I wanted
more out of life.

I knew I didn't want to just sail through life on autopilot or live
a different life in reality, than the one I lived in my head. I also knew that
I wanted to be different from the crowd and not just follow the same
*college --➔ job --➔ mortgage --➔ car loan --➔ better job --➔ bigger house --➔
bigger car --➔ retirement* route that everyone else did.

I wanted to do things, see places and really *live* life.

Perhaps part of this driving passion was because I had grown up
watching my parents pretty much do anything *but* live life. But even
though it would take years for me to actually circle back around to that
list and do something about it, the realization still came a lot sooner than
it would have (if ever), had I not gone through everything I did.

I probably would've just continued on the same path ... and even though
I still wasn't doing the whole 9-to-5 corporate thing, I probably would
have if the right offer had come along *(and then been miserable the whole
time)*. Or else, I would've just continued to work the hodge-podge of

full-time jobs that I kept picking up to support what I really wanted to do — which was to write for a living.

I would have continued to follow in my mom's footsteps and probably been too afraid to really go after any of the dreams or aspirations that I had, would have eventually picked up a gigantic mortgage to carry for the rest of my life and probably put off my *actual* life until "later," when I hopefully wasn't too old or too sick to enjoy anything.

And who knows, maybe I wouldn't have known any better and never realized that life could be any different.

But thankfully, yes … *thankfully*, I went through all of those storms. Because they are what opened up my eyes. Well, God opened my eyes. He used all of those experiences to do it.

Now, after surviving the perfect storm, getting rid of all the excess clutter, cleaning up my diet, cleaning up the products I used and finally getting emotionally healthy and letting go of all that old baggage … now, I am ready to actually *live*.

Or should I say, start "bucket list living," as I like to call it.

Bucket list living means going after those things you've always wanted to do … NOW. Not later, not "one day," not after the kids are grown, not after I retire … NOW.

Unfortunately, even the concept of a bucket list itself has become something that often gets pushed off until "later." We're all running around so busy, doing things that half the time don't even really matter, that we don't even have time to sit down and figure out what our dreams actually are.

It's a novelty … a luxury … something only rich people and celebrities get to think about. Except that I say that shouldn't be and actually *isn't* the case.

Of course, the majority of us can't just go around marking things off our bucket list full time and do nothing else. We have to make a living for ourselves and our families. But, what I'm getting at here is a *mindset shift*.

It's about realizing that you can start bucket list living, right now, within your current schedule, your current lifestyle and your current budget. You may not be able to fast forward right to the African safari (*or maybe you can, if you have the right connections!*). But, you *can* start accomplishing some of the smaller things right now.

Maybe you've always wanted to take a cooking class, learn to ride a horse or even just learn to make your own bread from scratch (*all 3 from my own list*). Those are things that you can start working into your life right now by making some small changes to your existing schedule and budget.

Don't believe me?

Try tracking your time and money for a week or two and see just how many "pockets" there are of available hours and dollars … hours lost surfing Facebook or watching Netflix, or money spent on expensive drinks every day at a certain coffee shop.

It's about making a few small changes to your lifestyle and, more importantly, to your priorities so you can start accomplishing some of these goals sooner, rather than later.

This is what I did when I set out (the 2nd time around) to start bucket list living. Thankfully, I had already lowered my monthly expenses by paying off my car and all my credit cards. But, I still was able to find other areas where I could cut back. I quickly learned I would rather spend money on experiences or travel than on material things or unnecessary subscriptions or services.

I also began talking about my bucket list ... to everyone. You need to remember, you never know who could know someone, so ask around to everyone in your life — your family, friends, coworkers, acquaintances, even the clerk at the store. Not only will you possibly find a hook-up to help you plan or achieve one of your bucket list items, but you might just find a buddy to do it with too!

When I put my bucket list on my blog, I got lots of messages from my family and friends who had similar items on their lists and were excited at the thought of actually accomplishing them. And it works both ways — they motivated me just as much as I did them. Because we are all much more likely to actually go out and DO something if we know someone else is involved.

So, go out there and get yourself a bucket list buddy!

And remember, there are no rules to bucket list living, other than to be brave, don't wait and have fun! If you put something on your wish list and then later decide you don't want to do it, fine! Take it off! Or if you keep thinking of new things to add, even before you've accomplished the older items, that's okay too! Just throw 'em on there!

And don't worry about anything sounding strange or weird to other people (*I want to take clogging lessons, for goodness sake*). This is about YOU and the things YOU want to do. No one else.

So far, I only have a few things marked off my list (*I've been a little distracted lately with a pretty BIG bucket list item ... getting my book published!*), but as I continue to travel full time, while writing and helping people to de-clutter their homes and clean up their lives, I am going to mix in my bucket list too!

Which brings me to my last tip … keep your bucket list in mind all the time. Wherever you go, whether you're on a family vacation or a business trip, you never know when an opportunity to mark something off may arise. Or when a new idea will pop up!

As for me, I think it's about high time to be part of a flash mob. And if it just happens to be a clogging flash mob, well then, bonus points for me!

Chapter 11

LIVING A F.A.S.T. LIFE

If someone had walked up to me in 2006 and told me all the things that I would go through in the following seven years, I probably would have broken down in body-racking sobs. Or had a full-blown panic attack.

We can never know what is just around the corner — good or bad. And I think that's actually a blessing, because it would be too much for us to bear if we did know.

But if that same future-predicting person had then told me back then that I would come out the other side of those storms feeling more blessed, more joyful, more grateful and more peaceful than I ever had before in my life, I would've probably called the men in the white coats on them right then and there.

It simply doesn't seem possible, does it?

How can you go through loss, grief, tragedy, trauma, fear, confusion, defeat, depression, anxiety, sadness, anger and illness ... and still be grateful at the other end? How can you be *more* grateful than you ever were before?

I don't know how exactly. But I am here to tell you that it *is* possible.

I know this to be true because I've lived it. And just like anything else that I've been blessed enough to survive, I felt the urge — the responsibility — to share it with all of you, so you know that it's possible for you too.

We all have different storms in life and yours will be different from mine. But the underlying theme is the same — you *can* get through it. You *will* get through it. There *will* come a time when you will stop just surviving and start living again.

And the amazing thing is, life can be even more abundant and more fabulous than it was before.

Do I wish I still had my mom here with me? Of course. Would I have preferred not to go through the trauma of an abusive relationship or dealt with the frustration and inconvenience of adrenal fatigue? A resounding yes and yes!

But while none of these things defined me, they *have* shaped me into who I am today.

You know the old saying, "*You don't know what you've got until it's gone?*"

I think that is true to a certain extent. I can look back on old pictures of myself prior to 2006 and still feel some longing feelings for those more "innocent" days when the proverbial poo hadn't hit the fan yet.

But I also know that now, *because* of all the loss I experienced, I am able to be truly grateful for the good things in my life while I have them.

Like I say all the time … it's like the blinders have been taken off and now I can see things more clearly than I ever had before.

Of course, I wish I could go back in time and have the "old" me see things for what they were back then, but it's better late than never.

Now, I am walking through life awake. Aware.

I am no longer tied down by material possessions or emotional baggage. All of the "excess" has been stripped away so I can focus my time and energy on what really matters.

In place of things, I have experiences.

In place of jealousy, I have gratitude.

In place of fear, I have faith.

In place of longing, I have contentment.

In place of chaos, I have peace.

I want to live simply, so I can live more fully. I want to take good care of my body, not because a doctor's report or a wellness guru tells me to, but because I want to put the best in, so I can get the best out.

I want to be the person I was created to be *now*, not later. Because we never know much time we have left.

And I want to help others get to that place too, because we're all in this together and, sometimes, you need a little help finding your way.

Life isn't about how much money you have in your bank account, how wrinkle-free your forehead is or that you have the latest version of iPhone before everyone else.

It's about so, so much more.

So my hope for you, friend, is that your life changes *now*, before the storm hits. That it doesn't take a tragic loss or a chronic illness to take the blinders off. That you can stop just surviving and start truly *living*.

Because that's what a "*F.A.S.T.*" life is all about … living fabulously, abundantly, simply and maybe even tiny (I highly recommend it!).

So, what are you waiting for?

Your life is waiting for you. Now go out there and live it.

ABOUT THE AUTHOR

Jenn Baxter is an accomplished author, speaker and freelance writer based in Charlotte, North Carolina. She has been published in numerous print and online publications and appears at tiny house festivals, healthy living festivals and private engagements across the country, speaking on the subjects of downsizing and mini-malism, clean eating, healthy living, and spiritual health. She is a regular guest on the NBC morning show Charlotte Today on WCNC-TV and has also appeared as a guest on several tiny house-themed podcasts, including the Tiny House Podcast and Tiny House Canada.

In 2015, Jenn launched her website, *Live a F.A.S.T. Life (www.LiveAFastLife.com)*, based on her own experiences with clean living and downsizing into a 160-square-foot tiny house. She now teaches others how to make similar changes in their own lives through her online webinars and her e-course collection, *De-Clutter, De-Tox, De-Stress* (www.declutterdetoxdestress.com). Jenn is the inaugural recip-ient of the Silver Tree Communications Book Publishing Award.

Connect with Jenn and follow her insights at:

www.LiveAFastLife.com
www.DeclutterDetoxDestress.com

Email:	info@liveafastlife.com
Facebook:	@jennbaxterwrites
Twitter:	@_LiveaFastLife
Instagram:	liveafastlife
Pinterest:	LiveaFastLife
LinkedIn:	https://www.linkedin.com/in/jenn-baxter-52074a22/

87567090R00089

Made in the USA
Columbia, SC
16 January 2018